Women in the Contemporary Society

By the Same Author

Women's Movement in Manipur

About the Author

Thokchom Binarani Devi, M.A. Political Science, M.Phil. and Ph.D., is an Associate Professor in Political Science Department of G.P. Women's College, Government of Manipur. She is the author of "Women's Movement in Manipur" published by Concept Publishing Company (P) Ltd., Dr. Th. Binarani Devi guided two Ph.D. Scholar in the Department of Political Science, Manipur University and She had contributed articles in books, journals (national and international).

Women in the Contemporary Society

Issues and Challenges

Th. Binarani Devi

CONCEPT PUBLISHING COMPANY PVT. LTD.
NEW DELHI-110059

ISBN-13: 978-93-5125-295-5

First Published 2017

Published and Printed by

Concept Since 1974

Concept Publishing Company Pvt. Ltd.
Regd. Office:
A/15-16, Commercial Block, Mohan Garden,
New Delhi-110059 (INDIA)
Phones : 25351460, 25351794, *Fax* : 091-11-25357109
Email : publishing@conceptpub.com
Website: www.conceptpub.com.

Cataloging in Publication Data—DK Courtesy: D.K. Agencies (P) Ltd. <docinfo@dkagencies.com>

Binarani Devi, Thokchom, author.
Women in the contemporary society : issues and challenges / Th. Binarani Devi.
pages cm
Includes bibliographical references and index.
ISBN 9789351252955

1. Women in development—India, Northeastern. 2. Women—Political activity—India, Northeastern. 3. Women—India, Northeastern—Social conditions. I. Title.

HQ1742.B56 2017 DDC 305.420954 23

Preface

The main features of Indian Civilization focused the non-coercive nature, political hegemony, mendicantism, national political control, tributary mode of governance within the Federal structure, and predominance/disguise of convention and customary laws. The liberal democratic Constitution of India opened up the floodgate, introduced different provisions in the name of welfare and development of the society, and the women are empowered to take in the socio-economic and political processes. Women could to some extent position themselves in the political spheres at different levels, even though the numerical strength is so low; and though this could not substantially reverse the existing status of the women in this country. While it is very important to involve them in the process of development, with the provisions of liberty, equality with equity, and justice, and to understand the interrelations between development and power relationship of all sections of people not only in theory but in practical fields too.

In the way for development of any society, issues and problems are witnessing from any angle with or without any notice. The problems and issues of the society started right from the family level and involved the whole human environment and again affected the entire civil society in which women are not excluded. Because of gender sensitization, women got themselves involved in different kinds and types of movements, either to express their views and opinions or free themselves from the numerous shackles of life as well as to protect and safeguard their dignity as women. On the bases of these issues and other facts of life, today women are no longer remained within the confines of tradition, custom and culture inherited by generation after generation. They moved out or are forced to do so to find ways and means to improve their status by deciding for themselves and do not wait any longer for others to decide their future; and not only for themselves they could not remain as a mere spectator in this decaying social scenario. Their areas of activities and actions spread far and wide, and because of this, the civil society can no longer remain as an onlooker to the women's issues and problems; it has to address and listen to their opinions and expressions. Sometimes, the issues of women and their movements are politicized by political and social elites according to their needs.

Discrimination of women and violence against them on the bases of the marginalization of these women and feminization of poverty are now at the centre stage on women issues. This arises from the increasing proportion of women among the poor due to several factors. These factors are insecure land tenure, poor access of basic social needs like health and education and effects of various forms of discrimination against women.

Present book, entitled "Women in the Contemporary Society: Issues and Challenges" is a comprehensive document which sincerely attempt at not only the present position and status of women and improving their place in the society, as an active contributor towards economically viable projects, but also as an integral force in propelling the workforce of rural, less privileged women to the forefront of our economy, to an acceptable and respected place in the social and political structure of the country. And most important of all, it is a humble submission to show women as individuals of an independent India, in general and particularly women of the backward and under-developed States like Manipur, with an ever-increasing sense of dignity and self-worth which will spur them or to contribute within an over increasing ambience of diligence and economic viability and ongoing political processes. Many social stigmas are heaped upon women for no fault of their own, only violent action towards them, and injustice. Then, again, denial of property rights, lower wages, violence in civil life, gender discrimination etc. are some of the notable social diseases that are exhibiting in this modern developing societies.

The first chapter of the book is the "Introduction". In this chapter, the real position of women in this society is trying to depict in a brief way. Different issues of women which are happening in this society are, mainly, the result of the gender discrimination—power and powerlessness, relationship between male and female. Different challenges are coming up. Actions have been taken up by the respective governments from time-to-time. In spite of the different steps taken up by the Governments, NGOs, private individuals etc., the issues of women in this contemporary society is on the rise. In such social conditions women are not in silent. There are no such activities or areas where the women folk are not intruded into, that may be starting from the minute household chores to this new modern scientific IT world.

The second chapter of this book is entitled "Gender and Social Equality". Social hierarchy, social inequality and social exclusion are internalized in the minds of the people. Due to such relationship between men and women, issues of gender discriminations are witnessing by the people. There was a stage of complete destruction/confusion of the society due to such type of discriminations. In Europe, with the beginning of nineteenth century there is a shifting or challenge of social hierarchy and inequality to equality, fraternity and justice within the framework of democracy. These steps spread to other secular democratic countries including India. As an independent democratic country, the Government of India introduced different policies and programmes for the transformation or shifting of inequality to equality within the framework of the Constitution. From the side of the public too protest movements launched against the social hierarchy, for making policy of social inclusion for all sections of the society. The issues of gender inequality and discrimination are related to social and economic structure, which may be based on informal norms and practices of the respective society. Gender relations are relations of dominance and subordination with elements of cooperation, force and violence sustaining them.

"Human Development and Violence Against Women" is the third chapter of the book. The issues of women in this modern society are multifaceted. It spreads just like wildfire; control certain issues in certain places, start another in another place at the same time or other. But as a matter of fact, the issue of women is not the issue of women only; it is the issue of the whole human kind. It reflects, again, not only to the human kind but also other environments which are related with human kind. The physical and mental violence women experience, and their need to gain respect within their own family and society have been obscured in other politicized issues. As a result the over-imposed power to men and subordinate nature of women; we are witnessing a number of socio-economic crises in all parts of the globe. Gender-based violence encompassed a wide range of human rights violation, including sexual abuse of children, rape, domestic violence, sexual assault and harassment, trafficking of women and girls and several harmful traditional practices. Anyone of these abuses can leave deep psychological scars, damage the health of women and girls in genera, including their reproductive and sexual health, and in some instances, result to death. Development is an integral process of social, economic and political transformation which implies the humanization of the living and working conditions for both sexes within this context, the promotion of the status and role of women in development should highly be solicited. Under a democratic system, the dignity of the human self is recognized irrespective of male-female distinction. Human development covered the freedom with all the growth and development of human capabilities.

With a strict patriarchal psyche, decisions are meant to be taken by men only and followed by women. While politics is essentially an art of acquiring and co-exercising power—the power to effectively influence by decision-making process and policies and implementing desired changes. The active participation of women in the decision-making process is of vital importance as there are good reasons to believe that issues affecting women are not given adequate scope in public life. The concept of women empowerment is empowering women socially, economically and politically, so that, they can break away from male domination and claim equally with them. Unluckily, in India with enough provision for socio-economic and political justice and equality, failed to take adequate measures in emancipating and empowering women mainly because most individuals and/or political parties who control various organs of the state are intoxicated with patriarchal values. The fourth chapter of the book—"Politics and Women Empowerment" tries to depict a clear picture of the real position of women by analyzing the provisions for women empowerment and equality in terms of political processes within the framework of the Constitution.

"Electoral Politics and Women" is the fifth chapter of the book. As a continuation of the above chapters, this chapter also tries to show the real position/status of women along with their way of political participation in the Indian society. Women are associated with qualities like docile, submissiveness, protected etc., while rationality, self-discipline, competitive, universality etc. are expected to be embodied with men by the Indian culture. This stereotype role between male and female leads to the marginalization of women in the political fields. Women are culturally assigns the responsibility of primarily parenting and nurturing—accordingly developed a psychological make up and choose the role of 'care giver' and prefer to confine them at home. Consequently, the numerical strength of the women legislators is unable to increase women's participation in local level political institutions like village *panchayats* and municipal bodies has also remained insignificant in spite of the reservation policy of the Government. The experience of India's sixty seven years periodic elections shows the inability of parties to make a place for the women. At the same time, the manifestos of all political parties contain promises of taking up programmes for the welfare of women. Simply, the issues of women become one of the important topics for capturing power through election. In accordance with the changed circumstances, the parties have established regular party forums, cells etc. for mobilizing women and seeking their supports, e.g. formation of Mahila Congress, Mahila Morchas etc. However, in the present political process of entry into decision-making political institutions, there is growing influence of money and muscle powers, backroom dealings, communalization, criminalization etc. As a result, many women have left political parties and formed informal women groups. Even during the elections, the individual woman's performances are subdued by the choice of elders in the family—father, husband, brother etc.

The sixth chapter of the book is "Women in Democracy and Peace Processes". The democratic Government has a great responsibility to create favourable socio-economic and political atmosphere for the empowerment of women, making them capable citizens of the state to discharge their duties in a positive and rightful manner. But within the framework of democratic societies in this ongoing global scenario and sixty-four years after the declaration of Universal Declaration on Human Rights, people are suffering from the problems of the violation of human rights. Due to gendered socialization, women are not allowed to participate in the decision-making process and remained as silent victims to the discrimination, violation of their rights, issues of domestic violence, harassment which the societal customs and culture made natural happenings for women. Women, which have been relegated to secondary status is not only absolutely false, but is the result of illicit generalization. Their contribution is both in theory and practice. Women are struggling, demanding and fight for the just cause with any issue or problem from time-to-time and place-to-place. They are no more remaining as passive spectators. They are coming out and take a lead. In a democratization process, there should be an obligation for policy-makers and security forces to be accountable to the public for their decision and actions.

The seventh chapter of the book is "Globalization and Women Empowerment". In this economically liberalized era, globalization would result into empowerment of women with greater and multidimensional freedom and reliance on market mechanism, but when examined in deep the situation seems otherwise. The goals of poverty alleviation are difficult to achieve without the full and active participation of women, who constitute a large section of the workforce in the country. Modern industrial upsurge and economic reforms have proved discriminatory against women. A fallout of this industrial transformation is the increasing violence against women. The impact of transition to a modern economy has meant exclusion of an increasing number and proportion of women from active participation in the productive process. Women are commodified, made chief labours and are made instrumental enhancing the market for commodities. Atrocities on women at their work places, as well as, outside, which have resulted in rape, molestation including murder cited as instances of exploitation, oppression and subjugation of women. But women are the beginning of everything. On her side, she needs to understand everything, aware of all the consequences, be able to fight and challenge all those obstacles, to acquire all the knowledge in all-round her all the time. Empowerment is the important step necessary for these things. One of the biggest responsibilities of the empowered women today is how to synthesize what has been valuable and timeless in our ancient traditions with what is good and valuable in modern thought.

"Liberal Economy, Women and Corporate Social Responsibility" is the eighth chapter of the book. Corporate social responsibility is a process with the aim to embrace responsibility for the company's actions and encourage a positive impact through its activities on the environment, consumer employees, communities, stakeholders and all other members of the public spheres who may also be considered as stakeholders. The women entrepreneurs implemented the corporate social responsibility model beyond compliance and engaged in action that appears to further some social good, especially for women self directly and for the society as a whole indirectly beyond the interest of the firm and that which is required by law. With the growing awareness about business and spread of education among women over the period, women have started shifting from 3Ps (pickle, *pappad* and powder) to 3Es (engineering, electronics and energy) and other industries under Integrated Rural Development Programme. Women tend to be the primary care givers for children and elders. Their careers tend to be viewed as secondary to that of their spouses. But with the advancement of education and modernization women are exhibiting their outstanding role and contributions; the progress of the society will be more quickened. If they are included in the decision-making process and action on society and environment, through the transparent and ethical behaviour that is consistent inclusive and sustainable development, we can get the exact obligation of the corporate social responsibility, because they experienced the social reality.

Chapter ninth of the book is "Extremism, Human Rights and Women". In this chapter the author is trying to depict the real picture of the conditions which violate the rights of the people, especially for women. No one is saying that they are against the public but the problems of the people due to the violation of their rights are worsening day-by-day. The non-state actors are saying that they are coming out only of the problems faced by the common innocent people. The state actors are also at the same time saying that they are only for the public. So, the sufferers are only the innocent public as a result of the conflict between the state and non-state actors. The new economic system introduced by the government assured the overall advancement of the public. But, it creates a new social scenario, that is more worsen than that of the Marxian view of capitalism for the poor, marginalized weaker section of the society. Women, who are the more vulnerable section of the society, take up different steps in connection with the protection of the rights of the people in this conflict situation between the state and non-state actors. At the same time, both the state and non-state actors committed different crimes against women.

The last chapter of the book is the "Conclusion". Here, the author wants to say that studies on the rights of women and their problems should be taken from the individualistic and sociological point of view. The claim of the rights of women is a part of the society. There are no condition as stated by the individualistic thinkers that man can live without society, he (man) was an individual in his own rights; that for the security of his property, rights and life or for the attainment of some other goals, man created society.

Women participate in multifarious socio-economic activities, women who are facing a number of problems in the socio- economic spheres often form different organizations. But they face all the problems created by customs, cultures, and religions of their respective societies. Society does not remain silent; it is change from one form to another without any fix time interval. A massive social transformation or change had its inevitable effect on the sphere of political mobilization. When the women entered into the socio-political process of the country, they started to take over the right, justice, equality etc. They set down some basic norms like, equal rights and obligation for all Indian citizens without sex bar; no disability to any citizen because of religion, caste, creed, or sex in regard to public appointment to an office of power, adult suffrage, women to contest an equal terms with men in mixed general election etc. Consequently, women have the right to vote and can contest the election. Even women members were there in the Constituent Assembly of India. In political sphere, India's women in general and Hindu women in particular, stood in the forefront of every movement. Modern Indian women are objects of admiration by people of the rest of the world for the role they have played in the country's public life. The civil society protest movements organized by the women from time-to-time against unjust government decisions have impacted on the state policy in respect of human liberty. This may be reckoned as a significant feature of women's power. And women should actively deliberate on how they may be able to assert their rights in the political decision-making system.

It is my great pleasure to express my profound gratitude to my friend and colleague Smt. Lhingjahat Kipgen, who took all the pains for clarification of all the doubts during the development of this book. I take this opportunity to express my sincere thanks to the staffs of different offices of different departments who have given me all the related materials for this book mainly the State Election Office, the Manipur Human Rights Commission, staffs of the Manipur University Library Manipur State Legislative Assembly Library and Library of Manipur Secretariat. And again, I am giving my thanks to those office bearers of different governmental and non-governmental organizations who had given me all the information without any hesitation and giving me moral encouragement for such writings. Next I extend my heartfelt thanks to the Concept Publishing Company (P.) Ltd., New Delhi, especially Shri A.K. Mittal Ji, for kind acceptance and good communication regarding the publication of this book and for turning my simple write up into a nice book. Last but not the least I am giving my thanks to my family members, more especially to Kripananda and Priyalaxmi, my nephew and niece for their sincere support in all the computer works; for their understanding and cooperation during the development of this book.

Contents

List of Tables

1
Introduction

Society stands for the whole scheme of life and it is interwoven by different associations which serve different purposes to complete the whole purpose of life. It is a product of man's instinctive desire for association which finds expression in the aggregation of people having common interests and united together by what may be called "consciousness of the kind". The societal aspects of human aggregation are based on moral voluntaristic cooperative social processes. Coercive power, violence and conflict do not explain a major part of societal existence. Therefore, it is argued that it is the non-violent, non-coercive power and normative voluntaristic behaviour that explain the existence and continuation of human society. Humanism means that all people, without distinction of class, caste, place and centre of birth, colour, sex and any other artificially created debilitating impression enjoy equal rights and opportunities—have equal human rights. It is to this end that Indian democracy must move forward. In this exercise the role of women must be emphasized as fundamental.

Women are the most beautiful creation of nature, not having any lesser power. Social rights of the individuals, and of women, in the society, arise out of her position in the nation-state. It is determined by the closeness of contact between the individual members of the society; which again is decided by the common interests that these members enjoy. After Seventy years of Independence, when an evaluation of the progress achieved in India is made in spheres of social, economic and political rights promised to the citizens particularly to women in a positive egalitarian atmosphere, there is a dismal picture of the country and its people that comes to our vision. This is because in India, for centuries, women have been pushed aside from the path of development in the name of customs, traditions and religion. As a result, they have been denied opportunities for social, economic and political development. This has driven them to a lower status in society. As women comprise nearly half of the total population of the country this denial has contributed in no small measure to India's continuing underdevelopment.[1] An Indian women's role is defined with reference to her relations with others—first, as a daughter to her parents; second, as a wife to her husband; and third, as a mother to her sons—like this. Adolescence is a stage in which a rigorous rational is given for the differentiation between a boy and a girl, and children are impressed with the legitimacy and the inevitability of it all. The methods used are more direct and to the point. Instruction through examples plays an important role, as does in practical experience. From the age of ten onward children are strictly segregated according to sex, and the taboo on any physical contact between sex is emphasized. Submissive and docility, skill and grace in various household tasks constitute the virtue of a womenhood. The mother moulds her daughter to be a good girl, a good wife, a good woman, a good mother in law etc. She also instills in her young mind chastity, purity, dedication and devotion to her husband and relationship with others.

Indian mythology and religious scriptures abound in various forms of woman who are worshipped from time immemorial. According to different beliefs women are the incarnation of *Shakti*—force or courage; *Abhaya*—piety and comfort; *Swasti*—fulfilment; *Saraswati*—learning and culture; *Lakshmi*—wealth and property and so on and so forth. They have a character to be sympathetic and assuage the sufferings of others. They are now the legal citizen according to the Constitution itself. Unfortunately, in the same strain mortal women have been ill treated, abused, and violated—though they are supposed to fulfil all desires and demands of the man folk. A woman is a creation of nature and should be treated like a human being. Generally, people see women as a squeamish being, having no distinguishable personality.

We have built up society, which merely reflects the old, vicious nature of a patriarchal, sectarian, communal and oppressive social structure, left by three hundred years of colonial rule. We have tried to build a just and equitable society on the unstable foundation, on a set-up which believes progress and development. Therefore, the results are not that which were desired to be.[2] In India, women are taught to be submissive to their husbands and it hammered to their consciousness that whatever husbands do cannot be questioned by the women. The personality of an Indian wife is identified by the ideology of *pativrata*. No wife can contemplate to continue as wife without conforming to this principle in actual life[3]. *Pativrata* is a wife who believes *'pati-pratyaksha daivatha'* (husband is living God). By chastity and virtue and undiluted devotion to her husband, the wife also becomes a potential power with divine grace and whatever she desires can be fulfilled by her without any difficulty. *Pativrata* epitomes a woman's personality and this in turn reflects society's cultural value and norms. Both are inter-linked. This is ingrained into the belief system. People believe this to be the legitimate system and it should be meant to all people. Women are expected to be perfect wives and mothers only when one understands these convictions. Otherwise one cannot become *pativrata*. For a women he is not just a *pati* (husband), but also *parmeshvara* (God) too. The problem is that this servile mentality is perpetuated by women themselves. This attitude of women is clearly found even today. What is the real condition no one can say as it is a family affairs. But through media information with the issue of Narendra Modi, BJP's Prime Ministerial candidate of 2014 Lok Sabha election, and Jasodaben is clear example of Indian Womanhood. Shri Modi was a popular single politician before this election of 2014. The column of his marital status was always left blank during the filing of the nomination papers. However, in the 2014 election, he had duly filed the nomination paper by clearly mentioning the name of

Smt. Jasodaben as his legal wife and his family clarified the date of his marriage and other details. But the question which never asked is her whereabouts and vocation etc. Whether she had accepted the reunion or not, did she make sacrificed, if she was happy to be the wife of a Prime Ministerial candidate, or performing her *pativrata* and *patnidharma* as an Indian woman etc. As a matter of fact, the ritual of *pativrata, pati-parameshvara* and *patnidharma* in connection with husband-wife relationship in India is—pick, use, and throw; and pick again for man if necessary and woman should follow the steps taken up by the so call husband.

The Indian Reformers fought to remove social taboos which were oppressive for women and were helped by English law makers in certain cases. The Indian Penal Code was extended to support and protect women against offences by categorizing offences of particular nature as criminal offences, to be penalized by law. Equal right to employment and equal right to education were granted to women, but as has been pointed out before, social and familial conditions did not give them this equal right unequivocally and they continued to suffer from being left out.

Under the aegis of economists like Prof. Amartya Sen, Dr. Mehboob-ul-Haq, Dr. Muhammad Yunus and others, measurement of development is not only confined to economic aspects using economic indicators as GNP, but also extends to social well-being using indicators as the Human Development Index (HDI), sometimes described as 'a measure of human happiness'. As for instance, UNDP for the first time said that development should be understood in terms of PQLI (Physical Quality of Life Index) under which the indicators are per capita calorie intake counting of people of any country, literacy rate and mortality rate. According to the above economists women are powerful agents of social change. Investing in women's capabilities and empowering them to exercise their choices is not only valuable in it, but is also the surest way to contribute to economic growth and overall development.

According to Amartya Sen, the culture of modern India is a complex blend of its historical traditions, influences from the effect of colonialism over centuries and current Western culture—both collaterally and dialectically. Sen observes that external images of India in the West often tend to emphasize the difference—real or imagined—between India and the West. There is a considerable inclination in the Western countries to distance and highlight the differences in Indian culture from the mainstream of Western traditions, rather than discover and show similarities. Western writers and media usually miss in important ways, crucial aspects of Indian culture and traditions. The deep seated heterogeneity of Indian traditions in different parts of India is neglected in these homogenized descriptions of Indian culture. The perceptions of Indian culture, by those who were not born and raised in India, tend to be one of at least three categories, writes Sen—

1. **Exotical approach:** It concentrates on the wondrous aspects of the culture of India. The focus of this approach of understanding Indian Culture is to present the different, the strange and as Hegel put it, "a country that has existed for millennia in the imaginations of the Europeans."
2. **Magisterial approach:** It assumes a sense of superiority and guardianship necessary to deal with India, a country that James Mills imperialist history thought of as grotesquely primitive culture. While great many British observers did not agree with such views of India, and some non-British one's did, it is an approach that contributes to some confusion about the Culture of India.
3. **Curatorial approach:** It attempts to observe, classify and record the diversity of Indian culture in different parts of India. The curators do not look only for the strange are not weights by political priorities, and tend to be freer from stereotype. The curatorial approaches nevertheless have an inclination to see Indian culture as more special and extraordinarily interesting than it actually be.

Indian diversity has inspired many writers to pain their perceptions of the country's culture. These writings paint a complex and often conflicting picture of the culture of India. According to industry consultant Eugene M. Maker, e.g. traditional Indian culture is defined by a relatively strict social hierarchy. He also mentioned that from an early age, children are reminded of their roles and places in society. This is reinforced, Maker notes, by the way many believe gods and spirits have an integral and functional role in determining their life. Several differences such as religion divide the culture. However, a far more powerful division is the traditional Hindu bifurcation into polluting and non-polluting occupations. Strict social taboos have governed these groups for thousands of years, claimed by Marker.

Indian women lack personal identity. The statement conflates 'roles' with 'personhood' and 'personality', implying that a strong cultural focus upon the one, somehow denies other. The approach taken here is that concept of 'selfhood' and 'personhood' is culturally constructed. In collectivists-oriented society this involves a strong orientation towards roles— especially towards kinship roles obligations—whereas in individualist societies the pursuit of personal goals outweigh the importance of kinship roles and obligations. One's personal identity is, therefore, very much a product of socio-cultural factors. Those who opposed women's suffrage emphasized that woman was the ministering angel of home and maternity was her proper mission. The exaction of political life is inconsistent with the duties of child bearing and the rearing of families. Nature had not intended her for political life. Her participation in politics was sure to destroy the integrity of the home. If husband and wife differed in political views and supported opposing candidates, it might mean discord in family life. Moreover, women would loss respect and honour which was naturally due to them, if they got themselves involved in the mud and mire of political controversies. Their participation in public affairs, in brief, would destroy their qualities as mothers and home-makers. The opponents of women suffrage further pointed out that women had shown general apathy in public affairs, wherever they were granted franchise. They were unable, being physically weaker, to perform the arduous duties of citizenship and, as such, they had no right to demand the privilege of franchise. Besides, women would be guided by emotion rather than by reason in electing the representatives. And, finally, their interest in public affairs would last only until the novelty wore off.[4]

In religious matters and learning, women were degraded to the position of the *Shudras*. They were denied property rights and freedom. The Priests had no scruples in thus crippling their own wives. People to whom the ladies of the king's harem no less than the wives of the ordinary householder, were easily accessible, could not have had any great respect for their own wives. This is not mere conjecture.[5] Preventing inter-marriage was the most important thing among the Hindus; and with this motive they introduced child marriage and prohibition of widow remarriage. Women then enjoyed great freedom and exercised a voice in the selection of their husbands. After they had grown mature, it was futile to compel them to give up their immemorial rights. The easiest thing, therefore, was to give away the girl in marriage before they were old enough to protest. There was a danger that on the death of their husbands, they might violate caste restrictions and marry outside the cast, if widow marriage were permitted. The Brahman law-makers, therefore, decided that a widow should not marry. Children were coping and learning to accept and assimilate in this diversity.

In recent years, particularly in cities or urban areas, some of these lines have blurred and sometimes even disappeared. Important family relations extend as far as *gotra,* the mainly patriarchal or clan assigned to a Hindu at birth. In rural areas and sometimes in urban areas as well, it is common that three or four generations of the family live under the same roof. Because of their limited exposure to the developing world, the Indian women, till today, are crippled with social taboos, myths and are shy to get exposed to a broader world are hesitant to shun their primitive culture.[6]

Existing laws are not adequate to secure equal rights for women because there is inequality between men and women. Sufficient proof of this is the concentration of women in lower paying, menial, unrewarding jobs and their incredible scarcity in the upper level jobs. It is obvious that discrimination exists. Women do not have the opportunities that men do. And women that do not conform to the system, who try to break with the accepted patterns, are stigmatized as odds and unfeminine. In most Indian families, women do not own any property in their own names, and do not get a share of parental property. Due to weak enforcement of laws protecting them, women continue to have little access to land and property. In fact, some of the laws, discriminated against women (for some community), when it comes to land and property rights. The Hindu Personal Laws, 1966 (applying to Hindus, Sikhs, Buddhists and Jains) gave women right to inheritance. However, sons had an independent share in the ancestral property, while the daughters' shares were based on the share received by their father. Hence, a father could effectively disinherit a daughter by renouncing his share of the ancestral property, but a son would continue to have a share in his own right. Additionally, married daughters, even those facing marital harassment, had no residential rights in the ancestral home.

Crimes committed by juveniles have risen steadily over a decade of 2001 to 2011. Government has introduced different mechanisms and amends the Acts and Laws of the country for improving the condition of the younger generation as they are the pillars of the nation. Previously, the Juvenile Justice Act, 1986, treated boys under the age 16 and girls below 18 as juveniles; it is amended in 2000, Child Welfare Committee, Child Helpline, Juvenile Welfare Officer, Juvenile Justice Board etc. But the problems of juvenile are increasing day-by-day. Table 1.1 shows the surprise increasing rate of juvenile issues.

Table 1.1: Juvenile Cases 2001-2011

Sl. No.	*Year*	*Rape*	*Crimes*	*Arrested*
1.	2001	399	16509	33629
2.	2011	1149	25125	33887

Table 1.1 shows the fast increasing rate juvenile cases but the number of arrested child is not increasing proportionately. This is one of the clear examples of the failures of the government. Further, it seems that most of the provisions have been jotted down only on paper and not implemented properly. The call to treat minors accused of heinous crimes on par with adults is an emotional statement that emphasizes retribution over justice. It goes contrary to global practice, which emphasizes that adolescents are given more lenient sentences for criminal acts as compared to adults. There is a global consensus that adolescents below a certain age are incapable of committing certain crimes because their mental capacity or moral competence to judge actions or comprehend them is way below that a normal adult. This global consensus recognizes that crimes committed by juveniles are often influenced by negative outside elements, which sometimes overpower their still maturing minds and force them into impulsive actions. We need to ensure that young adolescents are not held criminally liable for their immature actions in the same way that adults are. Adolescents should be given a chance to overcome flows in their character, which may be due to a cruel upbringing and reform themselves. Such dark travesty of justice was seen in the Nirbhaya case. While about 18 years got death penalty according to Indian Penal Code, the rapist murderer who was of 17 years; 6 months and 11 days old got away with just three years in a remand home—minus the months that, as Nirbhaya's father has emphasized, the juvenile rapist was the one who tricked Nirbhaya into the bus and brutalized her with an iron rod, inflicting wounds that led to her death. Under existing law, this heinous crime will even be expunged from his record—as if it were in exactly the same category as a petty theft. Surely, this is not justice.

Development, urbanization and population growth has inevitably changed the traditional rural based economic activities of women. Many avenues are opening up beyond the activities of the farm, handloom and handicraft, marketing of home products etc., but the crisis is that works available in the traditional sectors are not expanding and the new works available in the modern urban sector are far short of the rising women's labour forces. Consequently, absolute marginalization of female workforce is happening. Again one of the most common features of the poor rural marginalized groups are on their migratory journey to the upcoming urban/city areas in search of new ways for their daily minimum earnings. With the initiation of the Government and NGOs micro-credit system is becoming a common fashion towards the women. There are women workers of Women's Working Forum (WWF) who work as weavers of cloths, mates and baskets, cigar or *agarbatti* rollers, food processors, either work alone or collectively in other branches. They work as agricultural labourers on farm lands or they work for their kith and kin. They are providers of their families, working in service occupations, i.e. *dhobis,* cooks, sweepers, water careers etc. They are integral part of the production process and contribute to the informal economy.[7] But, unfortunately, their contributions are not acknowledged or hardly acknowledge by the society even by their spouses. Women face another severe burden which is invisible to the outside world, i.e. domestic violence. It is marked by sacredness and poor evidence; and there are social and legal barriers to its preventions. Awareness of women's rights, universal and enforceable, is necessary to prevent such abuse and raise their self-esteem. Above all, economic independence is the guarantee against such abuse which is very difficult to acquire by the women. Rampant alcoholism among men results not only the low male contribution in the family, but created different forms of problems and confusions in the family. Such attitudes of the male members of the family disturbed to the daily routine works of the women along with the domestic affairs and sometimes wrong charges against the women are also happening. The assistance of the government towards women is also hardly reached to the real hands. So, there should be job oriented institutions and factories to provide employment of both educated and illiterate women and young girls. However, only making effective policies and programmes is not going to help. The governments must ensure that their policies and programmes are effectively implemented. Government will have to make the implementing authority more effective and totally accountable as we have seen that only due to lack-luster and casual attitudes of the implementing authorities and agencies, many good policies have failed to yield the desired results in the past.[8]

The problem of increasing violence can be analyzed from various dimensions to fully grasp its genesis forms of manifestation and ways to effectively combat crime and violence. For India to become what we want it to become with a modern, rational society and firmly based on what is good in our ancient tradition and in our soil, for this we have to have a thinking public, thinking young women who are not content to accept what comes from any part of the world, but are willing to listen to it, to analyze it and to decide whether it is to be accepted or whether it is dethrone out and this is the sort of education which we want, which enables our young people to adjust to this changing world and to be able to contribute to it. What granted men the power and more important, the authority to thus view women as objects, the power they wielded in real life—as fathers, husbands, noblemen, kings—and the access they enjoyed to education and the learning of the creative arts? In this sense, the male gaze may be said to represent the visceral, emotional and psychological expression of male authority, the crucial node in the complex network of relationships which characterize patriarchal society.

In the past two decades or so, social changes have led to Indian families giving education opportunities to girls, accepting women working outside home, pursuing a career, opening the possibility for women to attain managerial roles in Corporate India. In urban areas, Indian women participate in the workforce in impressive number. For example, in the software industry 30 per cent of the workforce is female. In the workplace women enjoy parity with their male counterparts in terms of wages and rules in the formal economic sector. In rural areas of India, in the agriculture and allied industrial sectors, females account for as much as 89.5 per cent of the labour force. In overall farm production, women's average contribution is estimated at 55 per cent to 66 per cent of the total labour. According to 1991 World Bank Report, women accounted for 94 per cent of total employment in dairy production in India. Women constitute 51 per cent of the total employed in forest based small scale enterprise. One of the most famous female business success stories is the Shri Mahila Griha Udyog Lijjat Papad. In 2006, again, Kiran Majumdar Shaw who founded Biocon, one of India's first biocon companies, was rated India's richest women. Lalita D. Gupta and Kalpana Morparia were the only business women in India who made the list of the Forbes World's Most Powerful Women in 2006. Change is slow, yet the scale of cultural change can be sensed from the fact that of India's 397 million workers, 124 millions are women in the formal sector. Gender budgeting is the allocation of mind regarding the contribution of women and how much they got. It is not a special financial allocation of budget for women.

The World Economic Forum (WEF) in its sixth annual report of the Global Gender Gap Index has ranked India 113 out of 135, with a score of 0.619. In 2010 India was ranked at 112, and in 2006 it was at position 98. Coming together with the UNDP Human Development Report and its statistics on India's low position of 129 out of 177 nations in the Gender Inequality Index, the WEF grading of India is not surprising, but is of concern. One of the most disturbing population trends this Census of 2011 has highlighted is the continuing decline in child sex-ratio (female for every 1000 males): 927 in 2001 and 914 this time around. This can undercut both social and economic progress drastically. The government must take every step possible to address it, from naming and showing states that are the worst offenders of providing incentives for raising girl children. But all's not lost.

Literacy in India is key for socio-economic progress and the Indian literacy rate grew to 74.04 per cent in 2011 from 12 per cent at the end of British rule in 1947. Although this was a greater than six-fold improvement, the level is well below the world average literacy rate of 84 per cent, and of all nations. India currently has the largest illiterate population.

Despite government programmes, India's literacy rate increased only 'sluggishly', and a 1990 study estimated that it would take until 2060 for India to achieve universal literacy at the current rate of progress. Again there is a wide gender gap in the literacy rate in India, effective literacy rate (age 7 and above) in 2011 were 82.14 per cent for men and 65.46 per cent for women. The low female literacy rate has had a dramatically negative impact on family planning and population stabilization efforts in India. Studies have indicated that female literacy is a strong predictor of the use of contraception among married Indian couple, even when women do not otherwise have economic independence. The Census provided a positive indication that growth in female literacy rates (11.8%) was substantially faster than in male literacy rate (6.9%) in the 2001-2011 decadal period, which means the gender gap appears to be narrowing.

Man has become overlords of women. Women are supposed to follow all moral rules of life while men are free to do as they like. The relationship in the family culturally defined according to the positions in hierarchical structures. The patriarchal ideology serves to reinforce their acceptance. It is a rationalization of inequality and subordinate position. Quite often this is legitimized through religion and culture. In India, it was worse from other countries. She was told to serve her husband and in-laws. But women need to realize her potentials. There are a lot of animated faces and animated voices. Women need to understand these things very clearly. The cruelties were so much like infanticide, child marriage, mental cruelties, that the atmosphere forced for some reforms.

We know that there may exist vast cultural differences in our world, but there is one common truth that when a woman dies, became disabled, is abused or goes hungry, it can profoundly affect each of her children, her family, a whole neighbourhood and an entire community. "Women have been the pivot of life and all lives have originated from the women's womb." Indian women, from time immemorial, have been the nucleus of home. The first and most important institution is home. Child learns everything from home by imitating his or her family members, particularly, mother, whatever it may be, and a home without women is incomplete. The human rights of women are judged in the type of the society we envision. We envision a society where we can act on our own behalf with dignity nd freedom, recognition that we have both the rights and obligations to develop our full potential and support the development of others. The need of the hour is not only to accept women's right of equality as natural and human, but also to be protected by State and international organizations. In fact, women's subordination throughout the world should be recognized as a human rights violation and with due account to those structures of oppression that intersect and compound such subordination. Full realization of women's human rights requires the elimination of all forms of discrimination and violence; and the achievements of equality for all women. Violence against women exists in various forms in everyday life in all societies. There are several instances where rape victims in any society do not report the atrocity committed against them for fear of physical safety. This speaks poorly of both—which is deeply patriarchal in its attitudes—and our law-enforcing machinery. Instead of enabling women who have been victims of sexual assault cope with their trauma, large sections of our society often heap indignity on them. Delhi is by far the most unsafe city for women in this country. But, it is not just here that women are vulnerable of crime, especially of the sexual sort. Women suffer the problems of violence and sexual assault in any part of the globe, even though the time and degree may be different.

The physical and mental violence women experience, and their need to gain respect within their own family and society have been obscured in other politicized issues. Power relations are woven into the social contract of the family. Sonia Gandhi, President AICC in her Commonwealth Lecture on 18-3-2013 said "globally women's voices are not being heard in key areas." In such a way if it is neglected the development of the whole society will be impossible. Women in Kenya, Guatemala, Brazil, and India launched different movements for the protection and preservation of environment. Chipko movement in India in 1970 is one of the clear examples. But the voices of women in climate change and global warming as well as the direct impact of environmental degradation and climate change are not taking into account seriously in different occasions. These movements are not only for the women but for the sake of the whole society. It simply indicates that when there is any serious discussion, problems etc. the voices of the women section are not entertain globally or women enjoy lesser value in the public platforms, not only the leaving aside of the problems of women.

Throughout the world, there are practices in the family that are violent towards women and harmful to their health. Physically, women need separate care but in spite of separate care for the women different actions of the family and society are harmful for mental and physical health of the women. Young girls are circumcised, live under severe dress codes, given in prostitution, denied property rights and killed for the sake of honour of the family. These practices and many others constitute a form of domestic violence, but have avoided national and international scrutiny because they are seen as cultural practices that deserve tolerance and respect.

Preventive measures against violence are as important as punitive ones. Both at home and workplaces, men need to respect women as fellow human beings instead of exercising power over them. When there is power imbalance in the family that tilts in favour of the male, it promotes the same in children who carry forward to the future, the inequality and injustice. Extreme inequalities in opportunities and life chance have a direct bearing on what people can be and what they can do that is human capabilities. Inherited disadvantages in opportunities is wrong for intrinsic reasons, it violates basic precepts of social justice. There are also strong instrumental reasons for a concern with inequality. Deep disparities based on wealth, region, gender and ethnicity are bad for growth, bad for democracy and bad for social cohesion. Hunger is actually the worst of all weapons of mass destruction, claiming millions of victims every year. Fighting hunger and poverty and promoting development are the truly sustainable way to achieve world peace. We can understand development as an integral process of social, economic and political transformation which implies the humanization of the living and working conditions for both sexes and within this context, the promotion of the status and role of women in development. Such development requires the maximum participation of women in all fields, not violent actions against them. This participation is a significant indicator of the dynamic progress and development of every country, of individual rights which also imply the full equality of women and can only achieved within development as a whole. Women also need to realize their inherent strengths. They have to face the reality and the challenges. Women have to free themselves of religious orthodoxy and superstitions. Prayer and worship alone cannot bestow peace and happiness. If other's benefit from our actions, it will be an ethical behaviour. Any harming others is unethical. Women have to exhibit their self-worth. They have to safeguard their dignity and rights. Nobody has the right to violate any women's dignity. Women also have to make their own judgements in a right way. In countries like India, which boasts of respecting and honouring women, have their own people and culture and customs who disrespect and torture women. In a situation like this, women themselves have to rise to save themselves. Women have to bring in the change by themselves. Women, too have their own share of the blame because they have remained silent for too long, tolerated too much. Nobody will liberate the women, but only the women themselves. It is often advised to shun evil, not evil people. Women have followed this dictum for too long. The morrow will come soon only with their own initiatives. In India, the political response to cumulative gender inequalities historically embedded in a stratified plurality society needs a policy of correction by breaking down of formal barriers to women's access to legal, political, educational and economic institutions assuming that this could bring about significant changes in women's participatory roles. Man had all through the ages, dominated womenhood, subjected their women to inhuman treatment and deprived them of their just rights and privileges. They could defend themselves against unjust class legislation only if they had the right to vote and their views got adequate representations. In fact, the admission of women in politics would introduce in political life a purifying, ennobling and refining influence that not only would tend to elevate the tone of public life and bring about more wholesome political conditions in society, but also would ensure better government.

Notes

1. Ghose, Chitra; Ray, Soma; and Chande, Chandni, 2002, *Opening the Closed Windows*, Netaji Institute for Asian Studies, Kolkata, p. 9.
2. *Ibid.*, p. 52.
3. Kunjakan, K.A., 2002, *Faminism and Indian Realities*, Mittal Publication, New Delhi, p. 19.
4. Kapur, A.C., 1981, *Principles of Political Science*, S. Chand & Company Ltd., New Delhi, pp. 428-29.
5. G. Aloysius, 2004, *No Freedom with Caste, the Menace of Hindu Imperialism*, Media House, Delhi, p. 59.
6. Bhowmik, Krishna, 2006, *Indian Women, The Ushering of a New Dawn*, Mittal Publication, New Delhi, p. 30.
7. *Ibid.*, pp. 18-19.
8. *Ibid.*, p. 25.

2
Gender and Social Equality

Gender refers to the social differences and relations between men and women, which are learned, vary widely among societies and cultures, and change over time. The term gender does not replace the term sex, which refers exclusively to biological differences between men and women. The term gender is used to analyze the roles, responsibilities, constraints, opportunities and needs of women and men in all areas and in any given social context. Gender roles are learned behaviours in a given society, community or other social groups. Their conditions, activities, tasks and responsibilities are perceived as male or female. Gender roles are affected by age, class, race, ethnicity and religion, and by the geographical, economic and political environment. Male alone should not make laws pertaining to the rights of women. Their active participation in law making is of vital importance as there are good reasons to believe that issues affecting women are not given adequate scope in public life.[1] With the report of the survey conducted by Organization for Economic Cooperation and Development, Indian women spent a huge 298 minutes on routine housework such as cooking, laundry, pets and home maintenance. They spend 221 minutes on leisure which includes watching TV, sports and entertaining, compared to 283 minutes for men. Again, Indian men spend more than 670 minutes (11 hrs. a day) on personal care—mostly sleeping, eating and drinking. Consequently, women are comparatively lack in the knowledge of the socio-political development of the country. While the male members considered it as the poor knowledge of women; and not considered about their discriminatory attitude towards women. Even before Independence, all the social reformers emphasized fully on injustice to women. Pandita Ramabai was the first to emphasize its repercussions on society as a whole. She elaborates the argument that men prevent women from acquiring knowledge at all costs, because otherwise the women would put a stop to their unrestrained behaviour and the men would lose their freedom and superior position. In order to promote their objectives, the men prepared *Dharmashastras* which propounded that women had no right to the study of the *shastras*, they should live with their husbands like servants, the service of the husband alone entitles them to salvation etc. and forced the women to behave accordingly. Similarly, men repeatedly write and speak derogatory words describing women as cruel, treacherous etc., and prevent them from doing anything constructive.[2]

The promotion of gender equality is of particular relevance for the development of a democratic country. For women living in poverty, the most important challenges are ensuring their equal rights, equal access to influence and services, freedom to make decisions about their own lives, a greater say in public affairs, and equality in property rights and family law[3]. Discrimination, subordination and oppression/torture of females are found in every form of social life. Large women sections are still illiterate and incapable to decide for themselves. Liberty, equality and fraternity are the pillars of modern democratic governments. But the practices and principles of the laws and regulations of the governments are found quite different to each other. Gender awareness should be built into the entire policy process—from development, and implementation of evaluation. The policy-makers need to be aware of the different social contexts in which men and women live.

The nature of gender relationships and the inequalities which they embody vary considerably in time and place, leading to geography of gender inequality. In those regions of the world, for example, where women's mobility in the public domain is severely restricted by social norms, and where households are organized along corporate lines with the control of family resources, labour and decision-making largely rested in the hands of the senior male, gender discrimination is manifested in extreme forms.

Social Equality

Social equality means that all citizens are equally tangible units of society and no one is entitled to special privileges. All have an equal opportunity to stand up and develop their personality. It implies no distinction in the social status of the people, because of differences in race, colour, sex, class or caste, that is, there exists no unnecessary social restraint which retards the growth of an individual and the realization of his ambition of a good and happy life.[4] Social equality is a state of affairs in which all people within a specific society or isolated group have the same status in certain respect. It entails equal rights, opportunities, obligations as well as economic equity. When we speak of equal opportunities for all, what we really have in mind is appropriate opportunities for all. The really important demand of the champions of equality of opportunity is that certain extraneous factors like wealth or birth or class should not determine or limit one's opportunities. As in operative principle, it means that each man should have equal rights and opportunities to develop his own talents, or to lead a good life and develop his personality.[5] Equality is much more than a tally of resources on a set of social norms. It reflects the mobility inherent in everyone of us. It is defined basically means equal rights for people regardless of what factors they might have that are different. It is because of they are human they must be equal. But in India as a patriarchal society, there is no social equality, again, as the society is rigidly divided into caste and free intercourse between different castes is a social taboo. Society needed the women in a place where she could not prove her social usefulness, she was abjectly dependent on the men—father, husband or son and it was only because she painfully aware of her dependent role, as an object of desire, a servile entity at the mercy of the husband and even female in-laws whom she served silently, and who were aware of her dependent status, as a machine for producing male children—legal heirs to husband's property, it was not only internalized this role that it was possible to perpetrate physical and mental violence to her. We have to realize that male power is effective due to the insertion of women into a certain location. Man can be made powerless only by rejecting the patriarchal and hierarchical gender axes. Women had been experiencing inequality in power relationship with men from the household level to the national level where they are universally underrepresented in legislative bodies, organs of government and local political structures. Women especially those with low incomes, tend to have less control over their time. These factors are closely linked to their nutritional status, the quality of care they receive and nutritional status of their children. Women are dependent on the men, father, husband or son. They are painfully aware of their dependency and their servile identities remain at the mercy of the husbands and even female in-laws whom they serve silently. They become objects of pleasure and are regarded as childbearing machines.[6]

India as an independent country realized the importance of women's development and enshrined principles of gender equality and justice in the Preamble, Fundamental Rights, Directive Principles of State Policy etc. of the Constitution. Among the specific legal measures initiated towards that end were the Hindu Marriage Act, 1955; the Hindu Succession Act, 1956; the Dowry Prohibition Act, 1961; Equal Remuneration Act, 1976; the Indecent Representation of Women (Prohibition) Act; the Commission of Sati (Prevention) Act etc. The establishment of the National Commission for Women, 1992 (to monitor the matters relating to constitutional and legal safeguards provided for women and look into complaints involving deprivation of the rights of women); passing of the 73rd and 74th Constitutional Amendment Act, 1992 (reservation of one-third of all seats and posts of Chairpersons for women in institutions of local governance, both rural and urban); the National Education Policy, 1986 (overriding priority to the removal of female illiteracy and laid emphasis on women's participation in vocational, technical and professional education) are some of the crucial steps taken up by the Government in connection with the development of women and pushing them towards equality with their counterpart—male.

Society can change where the roles dividing people, such as the division of labour or job opportunities, are shared more equally. In recent history many societies have passed laws that prohibit discriminations against people based on race, gender or age. These ensure that all people are treated equally by employers. Governments and other members of society. Many of these laws guarantee what are known as human rights. The laws that established a balance between the powers of a state and the individual rights of its citizens are known as human rights. Some human rights are accepted by almost all cultures and political parties, while others are still disputed, e.g. rights supporting political freedoms, such as the right to vote in election, are more widely accepted than those supporting economic and social freedoms, such as equal rights for women.

Social inequality has been a historical fact. Some people enjoyed the loaves and fishes, luxurious cloths and buildings, while others could hardly get a square meal a day. The idea of equality was formulated with an eye of remaining such social injustice. With the development of democracy, it came to be accepted as a free legal agent in the scheme of the state, the legal personality of each individual is equal to that of every other. It is derived from the supreme value of the development of personality—in each alike and, but each along its own different lines and of its own separate motion. But the central purpose of social development and social equality is the creation of conditions for a free and multidimensional development of men and women in harmony with interest, needs and goals of the human community. Men and women must, therefore, be subjects and not merely objects in the developmental processes, men and women have the possibility to contribute, to create their own reality, development implies satisfying both material and immaterial needs, the respect of human rights, equality and the abolition of all forms of discrimination and violence.

Gender Discrimination

Theoretically, gender hierarchy can mean the domination of either gender, but in practice it always means a hierarchy of male dominance and female subordination. A common aspect of gender relationship across cultures and histories is the aspect of subordination of women to men. Gender division is the social recognition and reinforcement of sexual differences between men and women. This might take the form of an unequal division of labour, reduced social opportunities or social discrimination. Although women have won important rights over the last many years, gender inequality is still commonplace in most parts of the world. While countries with equal rights, laws have improved women's access to politics, jobs, and property, women are still not equally represented in government and business, and are often paid less for doing the same jobs as men. Often force and violence are resorted to in order to sustain dominance. But modern society is pluralistic and dynamic in which democracy enchants people. Under a democratic system the dignity of the human self is recognized irrespective of male-female distinction. When we talk of gender equality, women emancipation, women empowerment etc., it caries meaning to the educated women who are aware of the modern ideas.[7] India is a land where the women are revered as well as abused. There is, therefore, no single image of womenhood in the classics. This makes it difficult for us to get clarity in understanding the status of women in India. The Tenth Plan made sector specific strategies for women empowerment including socio-economic empowerment and gender justice. Different programmes and schemes were adopted for economic empowerment of the women besides adopting integrated project for women. The most basic factor which inhibited women from being empowered till recently, was the attitude of society towards women's role and her place in the society. These social values and attitudes get reflected in the education and socialization of girls and in the institutional arrangements of society.[8]

Since time immemorial, gender discrimination, which continued unabated in our particular planet, was necessarily conditioned by society which had decided that men and women possess different traits and attributes. This particular concept of gender was vehemently advocated by ancient Indian preceptors who strongly believed that because of their vile and fickle nature and other sinful activities, women should be restrained within the four walls of the house. They should be given all protection and embellishment, but no separate entity whatsoever. As a matter of fact, in the early Vedic period, women were honoured at least theoretically more perhaps than among any other ancient nation on the face of the globe. Obviously, some digressions are there, as is quite inevitable in a primitive society, but the attitude and tone of the language in early Vedic period is of affection, love and respect, unfortunately, this ideal situation for women did not last long. Slowly and steadily, gender discrimination raised its ugly head, relegating women to a secondary position, subservient to their male counterpart. Theoretically, gender hierarchy can mean the domination of either gender, but in practice it almost always means hierarchy in which men dominate and women are dominated. A common aspect of gender relations across cultures and throughout recent history is the subordination of women to men. Gender relations, therefore, are relations of dominance and subordination with elements of cooperation, force and violence sustaining them. This is so because most societies are patriarchal or male dominated. If gender inequality is part and parcel of the poverty and discrimination in a society, it must figure just as integrally in the set of measures to eradicate this condition.[9]

Gender identity results from an almost infinite series of cues derived from experienced with family members, teachers, friends, and co-workers and from cultural phenomena. Physical characteristics derived from a person's biological sex interrelated with an intricate system of stimuli including rewards and punishment and parental gender labels, to establish gender identity. Related to, and in part derived from, gender identity is gender role behaviour. Gender role behaviour is constituted by all those things that a person says or does to disclose himself or herself as having the status of a boy or man, girl or women respectively. If there were no differences between girls and boys, and all girls and all boys everywhere behave more or less in the same way, one could argue that gender roles are on sex, but as we have seen that is not the case. Not just qualities and characteristics, but even spaces are gendered. The kitchen or public well is entirely a female space. It is lose to find a social space that is exclusive to women. Here, one notable condition is women plus women support system is likely to be failed with reference to certain cases.

It is assumed that women's work is supplementary to the family's income, for after all, her real duty is performed at home and anything else she does is gratuitous. Men's wages alone represent a living wage and their work is 'real' work; primary and necessary. Women, socially powerless and lacking the means to express themselves to beauty rules in whose making they had played almost no role. Fixed in a range of roles and ideals which served as veritable mirrors in which they were asked to view themselves, women learnt to recognize and accept these various beauty norms as their own. That is, they imagined them to be given, possessing universal value. The male gaze triumphed precisely on this account by establishing itself as a way of seeing and framing that is natural to the human eye. It may be found in all cultures. This is not surprising, since in almost all cultures, men, rather than women had access to learning and the arts. The male gaze treated women as objects. Women's beauty was an object for male creativity and imagination to shape, manipulate and transform. Men were driven thus to objectify women by felt notions of pleasure, gratification and desire.

As a result of such above mentioned over-imposed power to men and subordinate nature of women, we are witnessing a number of socio-economic crises in all parts of the globe. At the beginning women are internalizing their problems as their own. But it becomes a social issue now-a-days. Different forms of social evils which we can find in this present day society as a result of gender discrimination are sexual harassment, infanticide, foeticide, illiteracy, low paid jobs, honour killings, unequal property rights. Maximum front pages of the daily local papers are witnessing with the crimes related with fake encounter, extra-judicial killings etc. The rate of child trafficking illegally outside the state is on the rise. There have been no let up in triggering fake encounter, custodial killings and gross violation of human rights perpetrated by the security forces.

Unfortunately, the Indian Parliament has done very little to address the legal absurdities regarding sexual assault or child sexual abuse and the modesty test is routinely followed by all Criminal Courts today. For the last 70 years after Independence of India, there have been various piecemeal amendments to the penal codes define rape as penetration, narrowly read as penile-vaginal penetration, all other forms of sexual assault, penetration or not, are dealt with as outraging or insulting the 'modesty' of women. Child sexual abuse remains clumsily and inadequately prosecuted under 'unnatural offences', which criminalized a range of different acts, including oral sex and same sex relations. But these provisions on 'outraging modesty' cause tremendous injustice to many women. Other grave forms of sexual assaults, like sexual mutilation, are similarly categorized as outraging modesty or as causing grievous hunt or other offences. In the absence of law governing child sexual abuse, many cases of sexual abuse of girls have been punished lightly as 'outraging modesty'. Now-a-days activities have demanded that governments do away with the notion of 'modesty' as a legal principle. Ideas of modesty and honour have formed the basis for violence, including so called honour killing in many parts of the globe. But the laws governing sexual assault should be defined in terms of women dignity and bodily integrity. The Supreme Court has in fact recognized that sexual assault is a violation of a women's right to live with dignity, and it is time that this principle is embodied in Indian laws. The government should address the problem as it actually exists, not how it was perceived by nineteenth century British colonial administrators.

Conditions for Gender Discrimination

Men and women are sexually different, their chromosome structure is different. From this an inference has been drawn that women's capabilities, aptitudes, reactions, understandings, generally speaking, their dispositions are different from men. This inference leads to an ascription of gender difference. Sociologists have shown that all societies are stratified or divided into layers, based on caste, class, gender or race. As a result, some people in a society have greater advantages than others, leading to social inequality. Some basic differences between people may affect their place in the social hierarchy. Gender divisions are common, because of the different roles—men and women play in their domestic and social set-up. Other divisions came from attitudes of race or unequal distribution of wealth etc. What we have failed to see so long is that there is no one to one correlation between sex difference and gender difference. Gender identity is a social construct while sexual identity is biological. By overlooking this important distinction gender biases are being projected as being unbiased and biological given, resulting thus in an exclusive disjunction of either male or female and not both. Such a dichotomy leaves no room for overlapping of roles between the sexes. The upholders of the male/female dichotomy at the level of sex and gender define—men as rational, women as emotional, men as strong—both physically and mentally—women as weak and sentimental, men as theoretical women as practical, and the list of differences goes on. Having listed these differences a value judgement is added, all male traits are adjudicated to be superior and female traits to be inferior. The conclusion drawn from this is straight-forward—the mainstream consciousness and women consciousness should be subservient. A fallout of the way of looking at the state of affairs is to treat men as protectors and women as the protected. Women, however, have to earn her protection and retain her right to be protected by strictly observing certain prescribed behavioural norms. She must be docile caring, obedient and strictly conformist.

What granted men the power and more important, the authority to thus view women as objects, the power they wielded in real life—as fathers, husbands, noblemen, kings—and the access they enjoyed to education and the learning of the creative arts? In this sense, the male gaze may be said to represent the visceral, emotional and psychological expression of male authority, the crucial node in the complex network of relationships which characterize patriarchal society. Patriarchy is both a social structure and an ideology, or a belief system according to which men are superior. An analysis of the main institutions in society—the family, religion, law, political, educational and economic institution, media, knowledge system—demonstrate quite clearly that they are all patriarchal in nature, and are the pillars of a patriarchal structure. Under patriarchy different kinds of violence may even be considered legitimate. In fact, feminists believe that violence against women is not just persuasive, it is systematic in patriarchy. It is both a social structure and an ideology or a belief system according to which men are superior. Ideology plays an important role in perpetuating social systems and controlling people's mind. The subordination that women experience daily, regardless of the class we might belong to, takes various forms—discrimination, disregard, insult, control, exploitation, oppression, and violence—within the family, at the work place, and in society. The details may be different, but the theme is the same. Another factor for male domination or gender discrimination in the society is the custom, culture and conventions of the existing society.

Women, by constituting an integral part of any society and culture, are often underestimated and discriminated in different forms and respects. Many a time, the contribution of women is neither given due attention nor marginalized while formulating socio-economic development plans. Being characterized by tradition of sex discrimination and social stratification, the Indian women also occupy a place of subordination to men in many occasions. The status of women is key indicator to the progress of a society as well as of the country. They share distinct and equal footsteps along with the men folk of the society. In maximum societies, women had been considered naturally unsuited to political activity and had been formally or informally excluded from it. The legacy of this old belief, reinforced by unequal domestic division of labour not only handicap women in the pursuit of political office, but also prevent them from being active in political participation of any type of nature. Women need protection of their rights and interests. Male alone should not make laws pertaining to the rights of women. Their active participation in law making is of vital importance as there are good reasons to believe that issues affecting women are not given adequate scope in public life. Women empowerment is a process of social transformation, and it is the ability to mobilize the women themselves around self-defined concerned and priorities. The concept of women empowerment is empowering women socially, economically and politically, so that, they can break away from male domination and claim equality with them. It is generally believed that the responsibility of establishing social, economic and political justice/equality lies in the state. The Indian states, however, has failed to take adequate measures in emancipating and empowering women mainly because most individuals and/or political parties who control various organs of the state are intoxicated with patriarchal values. Until patriarchal hegemony gives way to gender equality and young men are taught to respect women and womenhood, and until our chauvinistic society accepts the 'freedom of a woman' without hurting a fake mechanism, safety of women will always be an issue. Moreover, in the contemporary era of liberalization, privatization and disinvestment, the state has abandoned the policy of welfare. Under these circumstances, empowerment of women is possible through voluntary action at the grassroots level. Along with genderisation of spheres of economic activities, the rational and emotional capacities of people were also genderized. In this sense modernity created for women precisely the conditions against which feminists have rebelled.[10] Women also need to assert her innate capacity at their best level. They should instill their mind that problem is their's so, they should be bold enough. Many women, despite having faced brutal trauma in the hands of their perpetrators, do not find courage to report on the incidents to even their own families, leave alone legal bodies. The fact that they do not feel assured of justice, adds to the problem. It is difficult to get cases registered due to family, society pressure, and the stigma attack to it. And the support system is not put in place for such cases to be registered. Here, again women plus women support system is quite necessary. Social equality, however, cannot be forced upon people by the laws of the state, unless the sentiment of equality produced great changes in our social habits and social institutes. If the sentiment of social equality is wisely cultivated, it is sure to make considerable, addition to the realization of social justice for which the world clamours now. But social equality is difficult ideal to attain.[11]

Conclusion

Despite efforts to ensure social equality in many countries, it has remained a big challenge and no society has been able to achieve it. The political equality guaranteed by the democratic constitutions in the form of fundamental rights, political rights etc. is not able to penetrate deeply in the social roots in spite of many policies and programmes of the government. The democratic Government has also a great responsibility to create favourable socio-economic and political atmosphere for the empowerment of women, making them capable citizens of the State to discharge their duties in a positive and rightful manner. Women who were subjected to various kinds of subordination and inferiority position due to traditional social norms, beliefs and practices, handed down from generation to generation depicting gender roles are called for to empower themselves from within and from the laws, enactments, policies framed by the government. Democracy promised them the enjoyment of equal political rights with men as candidates as well as voters in the electoral process and equal participation in the decision-making process of the State. But in all democratic countries of the world, women participating in the decision-making process are found to be less than men. The question is how this happens after so many covenants, conventions, passed by the United Nations making women equal with men in their respective constitutions? There still exists a big gap between what is written in the Constitution and various laws passed by the Governments and what is prevailing in practice. Although the policies and programmes of the Government seem to be quite useful and effective on papers, the Government must take necessary steps to implement these policies at the grassroots levels. The implementing authorities or officials are to be made accountable for every action they take. Because, in spite of all the efforts made by the political decision-makers, the long established beliefs and notions about female inferiority and the social prescription and prohibitions build around them have proved a hard nut to crack and as a result, women find it difficult to use the existing facilities to remove the hindrances of equality. Arguments for women seat reservation in the Parliament as well as in the State Legislative Assemblies are also raised from different quarters. A Bill on Women Reservation of Seat is also lying in the Parliament. But a consensus decision on this Bill is yet residual and the Bill has not yet been passed in the Parliament due to lack of commitment and political will. Political reservations and provision of jobs for some middle class women are not sound methods for empowering women. In the social life the bias against women and girl child has to be fought by social movements and by ensuring freedom to women from the oppressive social codes. Both men and women will have to work together in this direction, so, that human resources are not wasted or exploited by the brutal forces.

Notes

1. Chanda, Anuradha; Sarkar Mahua, Chattopadhyay, 2003, *Women in History,* Progressive Publishers, Kolkata, p. 118.
2. Thorner, Alice and Krishnaraj, 2000, *Ideals, Images and Real Lives,* Sameeksha Trust, p. 137.
3. Tyagi, Suresh Kumar, 2012, *Human Rights and Democratization,* Swastic Publications, Delhi, p. 2.

4. Kapur, A.C., 1981, *Principles of Political Science*, S. Chand & Company Ltd., New Delhi, p. 229.
5. A.H. Doctor, 1985, *Issues of Political Theory*, Sterling Publication, New Delhi, pp. 15-16.
6. Th. Binarani Devi, 2008, Women Emancipation: a Way for Removing Gender Discrimination, in Ray, B. Dutta and Ray, Asok Kumar (eds.) *Women Emancipation—Focus North-East India*, Om Publication, New Delhi, p. 327.
7. *Ibid.*, p. 326.
8. Bhowmik, Krishna, 2006, *Indian Women, the Ushering of a New Dawn*, Mittal Publication, New Delhi, p. 83.
9. Sarkar, Anchal, 2006, *Gender and Development*, Pragun Publications, New Delhi, pp. 34-35.
10. Th. Binarani Devi, 2011, *Womens Movement in Manipur*, Concept Publishing Company Pvt. Ltd., New Delhi, p. 202.
11. Kapur, A.C., *op cit.*, p. 229.

3

Human Development and Violence Against Women

Human development is about freedom with building up of human capabilities—the range of things that people can do, and what they can be. It is defined as the process of enlarging people's freedom and opportunities and improving their well-being. Individual freedoms and rights matters a great deal, but people are restricted in what they can do with that freedom if they are poor, ill, illiterate, discriminated against, threatened by violent conflict or denied a political voice. The most basic capabilities for human development are leading to a long and healthy life, being educated and having adequate resources for a decent standard of living. That is why the largest freedom proclaimed in the UN Charter is at the heart of human development. Different provisions of the UN Charter, Covenants, and resolutions of the World Conferences at the international level; and at the national level the Constitution of India and the laws of the country mentioned detail about the provisions of the freedom, justice, equality etc. which are the full embodiments of the human development. Under a democratic system, the dignity of human-self is recognized irrespective of male-female distinction. But still women, who are treated as second class citizen in certain areas, are suffering from different forms of violence instead of the enjoyment of the fruits of the provisions of human development. Today no one is or can be separated from violence. Everyone and everything suffers. Ninety per cent in today's deadly wars of the conflict situations are innocent civilians caught in war zones, most of them women and children, in fact, these innocents are fighting for the rights of all human beings. More insidiously, what is considered domestic violence is often elevated to legitimate war strategy. Rape has only relatively recently been condemned as violence against women. But it is only rape of one's own which is bad. In conflict and warfare, however, violence against the 'other' is legitimate. Global integration is forging deeper interconnection between countries. In economic terms the space between people and countries is sh inking rapidly—as trade, technology, and investment link all countries in a web of independence. In human development terms the space between countries is marked by deep and in some cases, widening inequalities in income and life chances. Human development goes within the members of the societies are as stark as the gaps between countries. These gaps reflect unequal opportunities—people held back because of their gender, group identity, wealth and location. Such inequality is unjust. They are also economically wasteful and socially destabilizing. Democracy is in crisis world-wide at the very time when there needs to be a renewed emphasis on democratic practice as the key to the attainment of twenty first century human security aims. Democratic matters for human security because well designed and inclusive political institutions and processes are the key to both preventing violence and managing conflict constructively, and because respect for human rights and public participation are essential for meeting human development objectives.[1] The basic purpose of development is to enlarge people's choices. In principle these choices can be infinite and can change over time. People often valued achievements that do not reflect at all, at least not immediately, in income on growth figures; greater access to knowledge; better nutrition and health services; more secure livelihood; security against crime and physical violence; leisure hours, political and cultural freedoms and participation in community activities. The objective of development is to create an enabling environment for people to enjoy long, healthy and creative lives. Human development embraces all these aspects.[2]

Violence against Women

By expanding the definition of violence, we can begin to recognize that our methods of relating germinate, perpetuate and exacerbate (our own) sufferings. We begin to see how, for example, repressive and exploitative regimes (structural violence) are supported through mechanisms of penetration, segmentation, fragmentation and marginalization. Women, as centres of politicized identities, are no longer silenced by patriarchal mechanisms of ascription. Women can and ought to voice their identities on their own terms; not only women, but all subaltern groups previously denied voices by oppressive systems founded on binerisms. A common aspect of gender relations across cultures and throughout recent history is the subordination of women to men. Gender relations, therefore, are relations of dominance and subordinations with elements of cooperation, force and violence sustaining them. This is so because most societies are patriarchal or male dominated. If gender inequality is part and parcel of the poverty and discrimination in a society, it must figure just as integrally in the set of measures to eradicate this condition.[3] Violence against women regardless of the nature of the perpetrator —individual, group, institution, the state or society, is a human rights violation and is treated as such whether in the home, within the family or outside of it. Violence is an action or policy or an attitude that causes bodily or mental injury and debars or dehumanizes a person. The violation of the rights of women is a human rights violation of her body and her rights as a person. Preventive measures against violence are as important as punitive ones. When there is power imbalance in the family that tilts in favour of the male, it promotes the same in children who carry forward to the future, the inequality and injustice. Extreme inequalities in opportunities and life chance have a direct bearing on what people can be and what they can do that is human capabilities. Inherited disadvantages in opportunities is wrong for intrinsic reasons, it violates basic precepts of social justice. There are also strong instrumental reasons for a concern with inequality. The physical and mental violence women experience, and their need to gain respect within their own family and society have been obscured in other politicized issues. As a result of the over-imposed power to men and subordinate nature of women, we are witnessing a number of socio-economic crises in all parts of the globe. At the beginning women are internalizing their problems as their own. But, it becomes a social issue now-a-days. Different forms of social evils which we can find in this present day society as a result of gender discrimination are sexual harassment, infanticide, foeticide, illiteracy, low paid jobs, honour killings, unequal property rights. Power relations are woven into the social contract of the family. Maximum front pages of the daily web, national and local papers are witnessing with the crimes related with fake encounter, extra-judicial killings etc. The rate of child (girl) trafficking illegally inside and outside the country is on the rise. There have been no let up in triggering fake encounter, custodial killings and gross violation of human rights perpetrated by the security forces. The so called 'abode of peace' can be a site of conflict, violence and insidious abuse of women. The global community has finally begun to acknowledge the extent of violence against women, especially within the family. Such violence is now being called a Human Rights Violation, and fighting such violations is a part of any Human Rights agenda.

Violence against women exists in various forms in everyday life in all societies. There are several instances where rape victims in any society do not report the atrocity committed against them for fear of physical safety. This speaks poorly of both—which is deeply patriarchal in its attitudes and our law-enforcing machinery. Instead of enabling women who have been victims of sexual assault cope with their trauma, large sections of our society often heap indignity on them. Delhi is by far the most unsafe city for women in this country. But, it is not just here that women are vulnerable of crime, especially of the sexual sort. The National Crime Records Bureau, in its report for 2007, documents that there were 513 reported rape cases in Delhi City. This was way above the number of cases reported in Mumbai, which stood at 171, Bangalore reported 62 cases, Indore 74, Pune 65 and Chennai 46. And this is just a count of those cases that were reported.[4]

Unfortunately, the Indian Parliament has done very little to address the legal absurdities regarding sexual assault or child sexual abuse and the modesty test is routinely followed by all Criminal Courts today. For the last 70 years after Independence of India, there have been various piecemeal amendments to the penal codes define rape as penetration, narrowly read as penile-vaginal penetration, all other forms of sexual assault, penetration or not, are dealt with as outraging or insulting the 'modesty' of women. Child sexual abuse remains clumsily and inadequately prosecuted under 'unnatural offences', which criminalized a range of different acts, including oral sex and same sex relations. But these provisions on 'outraging modesty' cause tremendous injustice to many women. Other grave forms of sexual assaults, like sexual mutilation, are similarly categorized as outraging modesty or as causing grievous hunt or other offences. In the absence of law governing child sexual abuse, many cases of sexual abuse of girls have been punished lightly as 'outraging modesty'. Now-a-days activities have demanded that governments do away with the notion of 'modesty' as a legal principle. Ideas of modesty and honour have formed the basis for violence, including so called honour killing in many parts of the globe. But the laws governing sexual assault should be defined in terms of women dignity and bodily integrity. The Supreme Court has in fact recognized that sexual assault is a violation of a woman's right to live with dignity, and it is time that this principle is embodied in India's laws. The needs for this present social scenario of India regarding sexual assault recognizing its different forms and the varying degrees of psychological and physical harm it causes. Dangerously outdated notions of modesty should no longer be the basis for protecting Indian women and girls from sexual assaults. The Government should address the problem as it actually exists, not how it was perceived by nineteenth century British colonial administrators.

Different Ways of Violence against Women

As mentioned by Galtung, we can discuss violence into three different ways—direct violence, cultural violence, and structural violence.

Direct violence includes verbal and physical intended aggression against body, mind and spirit, included all forms of domestic violence, rape, sexual violence etc.

Cultural violence is a collection of mechanisms to legitimize, protect and sustain direct and structural violence, usually, through icons as national flags and anthems, media representations supporting prejudices.

Structural violence refers to mere enduring and less physically visible form of violence—personal, domestic, community and societal—that are provoked by unequal power relations within social structures. This includes such 'unintended'. Violence as poverty, starvation, spread of preventable diseases and human rights violations.

Women's Rights are Human Rights

The Universal Declaration of Human Rights defines specific rights—civil and political as well as economic, social and cultural with equality and freedom from discrimination as a principle and recurrent theme. It spells out the rights to life, liberty and security of person, to fair trial. Not only to protect the human rights, it shows the lights for how to protect the basic rights of the human beings, i.e. by giving punishment and how to develop the whole human world. Women could play an important role in the development process; the need of improving the status of women was felt accordingly, the General Assembly proclaimed 1975 as International Women's Year. In 1975 first world conference of the International Women's Year was held at Mexico City, where three themes—equality, development and peace were emphasized. The Constitution of India also lays down some provisions for the enforcement of the fundamental rights guaranteed by the Constitution. Clause 3 of the Article 15 provides that this would not prevent the step from making special provision for opportunity in the public employment, education, exercise of political rights, and enjoy same freedom and same kind of judicial protection in case of infringement of any rights. The National Human Rights Commission and Manipur State Human Rights Commission and a number of voluntary organizations are working for the protection of human rights against all forms of discriminations at the national and state level.

In spite of the Universal Declaration of Human Rights under the United Nations Organization and the Constitutional safeguards in India, women are subjected to various forms of discrimination in every sphere, be it at home or at work places. Violence against women—in all societies around the world—remains one of the gravest and most common human rights abuse today. It thrives because of impunity, apathy and inequality.[5] "Women's rights are human rights", this famous phrase is a proclamation of justice and human dignity for women, because whenever a women is treated as inferior to a man she is also being treated as somehow less human than a man. Additional international and regional documents that relate to specific concerns have been established over the last 50 years and above. There have been broadly speaking three phases in the development of women's human rights.[6]

The first phase was based on ensuring that women had equal political rights such as the right to vote and the right to hold public offices. The first generation rights are civil and political rights, enshrined in the International Covenant on Civil and Political Rights (ICCPR), which can be claimed by the individual against governments. These rights protect individuals from arbitrary interference by the state and are sometimes described as negative in that they require the state to abstain from certain acts such as torture or deprivation of life or freedom. These rights demand restraint from the state and that the state respects the autonomy of the individual but they are also very paternalistic and tended not to question and, at times, to reinforce stereotypes of women. An International Labour Organization (ILO) treaty during this period stated, that women should not work at night, presumably because this would be seen as clashing with their family duties. The main effect of this was to limit women's earning opportunities.

The second phase in the development of women's human rights occurred between 1960 and 1980, and focused on equality and discrimination. This phase culminated in the setting up of the Committee on the Elimination of Discrimination against Women in 1979, which deals with the State's obligation to eliminate policies that discriminate against women and then sets out different areas of discrimination such as political and public life, employment, health care, financial credit, the law etc. This is a binding treaty, which means that States that have signed up to it must abide by it. They must also make sure that people in their territories respect these obligations too (due diligence). However, for a long time women's rights were marginalized from the UN system and CEDAW operated in isolation from other UN treaty bodies, which did not integrate the rights of women, so for example the Committee against torture that were gender-specific. Things began to change during the late 1980s; there was an increasing move towards interpreting gender-specific abuses and violations within the remits of existing international conventions.

The third phase in the development of women's rights as human rights began in the early 1990s. Here we see the attempt to integrate in a much more systematic manner the issue of women's human rights with UN Human Rights Treaties.

A Khap Panchayat in Haryana recently earned itself notoriety by pronouncing that early marriage was the solution of rape. Other equally outrageous suggestions that are often made include the advice that women should not dress 'provocatively' which is tantamount to asking for it. Desirable indeed necessary, as all these recommendations are, they are *post facto* responses to these crimes, not preventive measures. The motiveless crime of rape—the only 'motive' of such an act of gross savagery being be demonstrated the male perpetrator's total subjugation of a woman by violating, both physically and emotionally, the innermost core of her being—is a morbid disease, a cancer in our society. And as with other forms of cancer, prevention should take priority over cure. Better and more vigilant policing of streets and public transport and other practical measures are obviously necessary and must be adopted with immediate effect to curb these heinous crimes. But all these will not help in understanding the psychology of rape, getting to the root of the concern which is not about the complete domination of the female by the male. Rape and sexual violence, including harassment, occur at different levels of society and is distinct settings. Although all forms are connected as manifestations of sexual violence against women, they are distinct in that particularized strategies are necessary in order to provide appropriate remedies. The Indian Forum Against the Oppression of Women has enumerated nine distinct forms of rape—1. Communal rape, 2. Gang rape, 3. Political rape, 4. Rape of minors, 5. Marital rape, 6. Army rape and police rape (in situation of war or peace keeping), 7. Institutional rape (in hospital, remand home, and persons), 8. Rape in economically dependent circumstances, and 9. Rape within political organizations.[7] The street, stations, subways, buses, autos, trains, over bridges, cabs belong to women as much as they do to men. We should reclaim what is rightfully ours, without being brow beaten into scampering away in fright. Why retreat at this stage? If anything, the moment to go ahead and change the rules of this dastardly game is now. If we weaken our resolve and move even an inch from the position taken, we shall have surrendered a basic right—the right to freedom, the right to safety etc. Worst of all, we will be passing on a nasty massage to our youngsters that all men are potential rapists—it is about opportunity.

These and similar pieces of advice which are an insult to the dignity and autonomy of women, make the common assumption that rape is a sex crime, motivated by eroticism. Rape has nothing to do with eroticism, not even in its most deviant form. Rape is the culmination of a deep seated hostility against the female gender that is ingrained in our society. Like *dalits,* they continue to be targets of revilement and humiliation in the most bestial forms, of which rape is only one example. If we are to rid ourselves of rape, we have first to rid ourselves of the systematic and inbred debasement of women which continues to prevail in our tech savvy. Thirty eight cases of sexual harassment were registered during the period of ten years against CISF personnel, out of which, a maximum of 13 were in 2008, 11 in 2007, six in 2009 and two in 2006 and one each in 2004 and 2005. With the coming of the Right to Information Act, corruption, harassment etc. are transparent to all people. But the only question is the solution of the problem, real judgement of the crime etc. as a part of the democratic norms people expect of the good and timely protection from the side of the judiciary. But in almost all the cases of rape/sexual assaults the activities of the judiciary is never satisfactory. As a last resort women, in group and individual launch different forms of movements.

In the armed conflict situation of Manipur many people are killed and kidnapped both by the state and non-state actors. Many newly married women are forced to commit suicide to save themselves against rape and social abuse by the security forces. With the increase of state violence in the state particularly against the youth and the women, the women community in Manipur staged unrobed protest march against custodial rape and killing of Ms Manorama by the Assam Rifles personnel on 11th July, 2004.[8]

The rate of violent action against women is increasing day-by-day with increasing number of population even though the Government (both Centre and State) have been taken up different steps including the establishment of National Women Commission and State Women Commissions. Regarding this matter the Chief Minister of Assam decided to increase the number of women in the State police department by the end of 2014. With reference to the report of the National Crime Record Bureau (NCRB), crime against women is increasing in Assam. The following Table 3.1 shows the rate of increasing crime against women in Assam during 2012 and 2013.

Table 3.1: Crime against Women in Assam 2012-13

Year	*Crime against women*	*Number of kidnapping and abduction*
2012	13544	3360
2013	17449	4000

Source: Media information.

The report also mentioned that 8,636 cases of cruelty by husbands and in-laws towards women are reported in 2013 only. There are also a number of cases which are not reported/ complained due to different reasons. Krishna Tirath, Minister of State (Independent Charge) for Women and Child Development stated in the Rajya Sabha that there are news for women and child trafficking in Manipur, but no record or cases filed regarding the matter is found in the National Crime Record Bureau. During the period of three years, i.e. 2007-2009, no case regarding the women and child trafficking is found from Arunachal Pradesh, Manipur and Lakshadweep. According to NCRB, the number of women and child trafficking during 2007 to 2009 are as follows in Table 3.2:

Table 3.2: Number of Trafficked Women and Children (2007-2009)

Year	*State*	*Union Territories*	*Total*
2007	3487	81	3568
2008	2580	79	2659
2009	2429	45	2474

Source: *Poknapham* (Manipuri local daily), 12.03.2011, p. 1.

Reports of missing children mainly girl children are there in the office files of the Non-governmental organizations and semi-governmental organizations. Those trafficked children are belonging to poor or victims of domestic violence. In many cases, the traffickers lure parents with promises of good education and food for their wards, and then take the children away to work in other states under inhuman conditions. Child Line, under the Coordinatorship of Mala Lisham detected most of the cases of illegal transfer of children from Manipur outside the State for the last few years.

Table 3.3: Number of Child Trafficked from Manipur (2007-2010)

Year	*No of Children*	*Destination*
2007	05	Singapoor
2008	22	Chennai
2009	16	Chennai
2010 (January only)	54	Tamil Nadu

Source: Media information.

Childhood is a period in one's life where one should be given ample opportunities to develop in a healthy environment. But there is a big bad monster in this happy story of childhood, i.e. child sexual abuse. The serious problem in this case is that many parents are uneasy in talking about it and this can damage the child, even though the condition became somewhat changed recently.

Domestic Violence

Domestic violence is a violent victimization of women within the boundaries of family, usually by men or his family to whom they are married or with whom they have marriage like relationship. It is also known as domestic abuse, spousal abuse, battering, family violence, dating abuse, and intimate partner violence. It is a pattern of behaviour which involves the abuse by one partner against another in an intimate relationship such as marriage, cohabitation, dating or within the family.

Domestic violence can take many forms—1. *Physical aggression or assault*—In many places, sex in marriage is constructed as the right of the husband who can claim it by force. It includes hitting, kicking, biting, showing, restraining, slapping, throwing objects, battering; 2. *Threat*—sexual abuse, controlling, domineering, intimidation, personality traits and mental characteristic; 3. *Passive abuse*—This type of violence covers neglect, psychological (genetic and brain dysfunctions), jealousy; and 4. *Economic abuse.*

Local customs and traditions are often responsible for maintaining certain forms of domestic violence including son preference, which can lead to abuse and neglect the girl children by disappointed family members, child and forced marriage, dowry and hierarchic caste system which stigmatized 'lower caste' and untouchable, leading to discrimination and restricted opportunities of the female and thus making them more vulnerable to abuse. It indicates threats or aggressive behaviour towards her not only to her physical being but towards her self-respect and self-confidence. It covers omissions and commissions, as well as conduct of a 'respondent' who causes harm or injury to the 'aggrieved person' by way of physical, sexual, verbal and emotional abuse and economic abuse. Coercion of an aggrieved person to extract any dowry, or other property or a vulnerable security will also be reckoned as 'domestic violence'.[9]

After Independence of India, the Constitution granted the equality of all the people before law and equal protection of laws. Women were allowed legal equality in all respects except family laws. But the marriage and family were not included in all the parts of the Constitution of India as done in Japan and other countries. Because of this, the women in India still suffering from different forms of tortures and violence in spite of the Acts and Bills passed by the Parliament. Mixed feelings have greeted the arrival of the protection of women from Domestic Violence Act, 2005. Women groups all over the country have been happy, if not exactly ecstatic, that the Government has at least come to the rescue of the battered women. The most crucial of definition is domestic violence embodied in the Sec. 3 of the Act. Violence against women—in all societies, around the world—remains one of the gravest and most common human rights abuse today. It thrives because of impunity, apathy and inequality.[10]

Women in this present day society are in danger if twenty first century society where being born a female is commonly considered to be a course. Women are subject to various forms of gender assaults, gross or subtle, throughout their lives. Rape is not an isolated act, it is a chronic condition. And it begins in the womb, when the female foetus is formed. And only too often she is killed for the sin of belonging to her gender. It takes one incident to galvanize people. Raped and otherwise sexually assaulted during times of internal conflict even by the state actors. Custodial rape is becoming a common happening of the day, and targeted for sexual violence based on their low social status. Nevertheless, many government actions in response to violence against women were inadequate. After the Nirbhaya Gang Rape case of December 2012, Government of India took up steps at war footing like First Tract Courts, Verma Committee etc., but the number of violence against women, especially rape and molestation is likely increased in every nook and corner of India, according to the media information. While some Governments focused legislative attentions on domestic and sexual violence, such reforms were undermined by structural barriers of women's meaningful access to legal redress and protection from further violence. Domestic violence victim face nearly insurmountable obstacles when attempting to report assaults. *De-Jure* discriminations, as well as customary practices, often kept women in a subordinate status in their communities. This unequal status made them targets for sexual and domestic violence. Violence against women further diminished and entrenched women second class status through impunity. Nobody can predict which that incident could be. What the Delhi incident of December 2012 has once again reiterated is that the next victim could be anybody—just about anybody—which includes people dear to you. In combating the problems of violence against women, the Government needs to understand that it is not merely a law and order problem. There is a social and psychological aspect to the problem as well. Certainly cases of rape and other assaults on women should be made for stringent. The convicted should not have the right to appeal to a higher court against the judgement of the lower court in open and such cases, especially in cases of gang rape. The sentence for such crimes should be upgraded to life imprisonment in all cases. The law enforcement authorities must be sensitized on how to deal with victims of such assaults, with more policewomen being inducted into the force.

Largely viewed as a private family matter, neighbours, friends and often even the wife's family rarely interfere in situations of domestic violence. Wives are generally regarded as 'belongings' to their husbands. Marital rape and sexual violence of the spouse are only topics of written documents. Thus, there is social acceptance of his right to 'correct' her if she had displeased or disobeyed him in anyway, howsoever minor. Normal standards of right and wrong are suspended when the victim of the abuse is a wife, indicative of the sharp divide between social perceptions of 'public' and 'private' spheres. So, prevalent is the existence of wife abuse that women who protest rarely find support, often being told this is a reality with which they must learn to live.

Maximum incidents of domestic violence remained within the four walls of their houses. Only few cases are coming out to the notice of the public. Number of cases filed to the Manipur State Commission for Women regarding the problems of domestic violence is increasing day-by-day.

Table 3.4: Domestic Violence in Manipur

Sl. No.	*Year*	*Cases*
1.	2007	27
2.	2008	45
3.	2009	19
4.	2010	31
5.	2011 October	102

Source: Manipur State Commission for Women, Imphal.

On Friday, November 4th, 2011, the National Commission for Women (NCW) said that the maximum number of cases of harassment of women were reported from Uttar Pradesh and Delhi in the past three months. According to NCW, it received 2,853 complaints from UP followed by 526 from Delhi, 372 from Rajasthan, 217 from Haryana and 139 from Madhya Pradesh between August 1 and October 31, 2011. The Commission received 1119 complaints of police apathy followed by 1105 complaints of domestic violence or matrimonial disputes, 326 property disputes, 181 rape cases and 158 complaints by in-laws. NCW Chairperson Mamta Sharma said the Commission has spoken to the State Governments for taking appropriate action in this regard.[11]

Women rarely report incidents of domestic violence to the police, believing that this will bring shame and dishonour to the family. Even when they do, usually only in serious situations, the police tend to treat incidents of domestic violence as marital disputes, and often refuse to register the case. Thus, the only time for cases of wife abuse receive attention is when they take an extreme form—nose cutting, burning, or other forms of heinous injury—a stage when serious damage has already been done. Even then, cases are rarely prosecuted with zeal. The same attitudes are reflected in the judiciary, which seldom recognizes cruelty as a ground in cases of dissolution of marriage filed by wives, and often gives lenient sentences to men in criminal cases involving domestic violence. In spite of the implementation of 'Domestic Violence Act, 2005' women are suffering from different forms of physical, sexual and psychological abuse in the private sphere and these actions are tolerated by the State and the community. But the actions of violence are becoming beyond the limit of tolerance. This condition was taken serious by Rashida Manjoo, UN Special Rapporteur, when she came to Manipur as a part her visit to India in the beginning of 2013. During her visit, she met with Sharmila Chanu and holds a conference at Classic Hotel-Imphal. She pointed out that the perpetrators included husband, in-law, and other family members. But these actions are brushed aside as a 'general remark' which are 'baseless' even by the Government including the police department.

Women's Economic Activities and Violence

The division of labour in domestic chores and childcare is rarely renegotiated across the genders. Despite their increased labour input into paid work, women (particularly married women) either continued to bear the main burden of domestic work, or share it with other female members of the household, often their daughters. By and large, gender inequalities in work burdens appear to be intensified. The attention to export oriented manufacturing and agriculture should not detract attention from an important fact of life. The vast majorities of working women do not work in these sectors, but are to be found in the informal economy concentrated in the most actualized forms of waged labour and low value owned account enterprises. There has been a great deal of controversy about whether labour standards including the right to organize, can be improved through trade sanctions. Whatever the outcome of this debate, however, the reality remains. Globally, enforced labour standards will do little to change the lives and livelihoods of the vast majority of working women in the informal economy where such standards are impossible or impossibly expensive, to enforce. A more inclusive approach would be to institute a universal social floor based on supporting all and supported by all. After the liberalization of economy and in the new circumstances created by SAP for globalization, the traditional role of women is being undermined whereas mechanization and automation is becoming prevalent in the market based economy which has adversely affected the village based traditional economy. The opening of markets led to the commercialization of agriculture and new technologies penetrated into our agricultural lands. The transmission of knowledge about the new technologies like use of tractors, high quality fertilizers, selection of HYV seeds, pesticides etc. became man-to-man affairs. Men were increasingly drawn into the modernizing agriculture sector while women stayed in subsistence agriculture with no access to credits, training and technologies. The agricultural development has normally and almost entirely been manned by men right from the decision-making to implementation.[12] Again women have also been excluded from owning or controlling land, even after the implementation of the Right to Property Act, 2005, the most crucial productive resource in agricultural economies. Earlier women and men were equal partners in agriculture. Their knowledge and contribution and participation in decision-making were recognized. But with the commercialization of agriculture, women's job is taken up by men and mechanization has displaced a large segment of agricultural work.

Steps for Elimination of Violence against Women

Accordingly, the Vienna Human Rights Conference and the Fourth World Conference on Women gave priority to this issue which jeopardizes women's lives, bodies, psychological integrity and freedom. Violence against women and girls constitute the single most prevalent and universal violation of human rights. The United Nations, in keeping with the spirit of the UN Declaration of Human Rights, work in many ways to eliminate this morally unacceptable scourge. UN Conference on Human Rights, the 1979 Convention on the Elimination of All Forms of Discrimination Against Women (CEDAW), the Beijing Declaration, the United Nations Development Fund for Women (UNIFEM) etc. are some of the instruments that would address the issue of gendered violence. Despite regard for the principle of non-discrimination in the enjoyment of rights contained in the UDHR, ICCPR, ICESCR, and other human rights instruments, women were not treated equally at the global level. CEDAW acknowledged that discrimination against women violates the principles of equality of rights and respect for human dignity, and is an obstacle to the participation of women, on equal terms with men, in the political, social, economic and cultural life of their countries. This in turn, affects the development of family and society as a whole. The Convention recommends wide ranging principles for eliminating discrimination against women-recognition of the fact that even after the Universal Declaration of Human Rights upheld the principles of freedom and equality, discrimination against women persists. According to this Convention, discrimination refers to any distinction, exclusion or restriction made on the bases of sex which has the effect or purpose of nullifying the recognition, enjoyment or exercise by women, irrespective of their marital status, on the bases of equality of men and women, of human rights and fundamental freedom in the political, economic, social, cultural, civil and any other fields.

A Conference on "Women Forging a New Security; Ending Sexual Violence in Conflict" was held on 23rd to 25th May, 2011 at Toronto, Canada. It was attended by the women from different countries of the world including women Nobel Prize Laureates—Myrid Magur, 1976; Jodi William, 1997; and Shirin Ibadi, 2003. Aung San Sue Key of Myanmar did not attend the Conference, but sent her video massage. In that Conference Binaluxmi Nepram, Member, Manipur Gun Survivor Network highlighted the problems faced by the women of Manipur and North-East India in this armed conflict situation and sexual violence in this region. Nobel Prize Laureate women expressed their sensibility and feelings of sorrow about the problems of Manipuri women. They have decided to urge for saving women from violence not only from the Government, but from the non-state actors too. They have shown their solidarity to Sharmila Chanu for her movement for the removal of the Armed Forces Special Power Act, 1958.

The Government of India made different Acts and Laws in connection with the rights and protection of women on the bases of the report of the committees which are formed from time-to-time. Establishment of the National Commission for Women, State Commission for Women, Women Development Corporation etc. are some examples in this regard. Different non-governmental organizations and agencies, academic bodies are also actively involved in the steps for protection of women from any sort of problems. Keeping in view the duty of the Union under Art. 355 of the Constitution, *inter alia* to protect every State against internal disturbance, it is considered desirable that the Central Government should also have power to declare areas as 'disturbed', to enable its armed forces to exercise the special powers. Areas declared 'disturbed' under the Armed Forces Special Power Act (AFSPA) over the past 50 years vary significantly according to their conflict history, ethnic constituency, and levels of militancy. However, all the areas where this act is imposed share a common experience of widespread human rights abuses. The AFSPA has also had the opposite effect in each State where the AFSPA has been implemented and soldiers have been deployed; the armed forces have become a symbol of oppression and an object of hate. Human rights violation has served to fuel conflicts and act as a recruiting sergeant for militant groups in many parts of the country.[13] Arbitrary detention, torture, and the killing of peaceful critics have had the effect of closing democratic and peaceful paths of opposition, forcing organizations underground and fuelling a growth in militancy. Not only from the side of the state actor, many militant groups have been responsible for human rights abuses, including torture, indiscriminate killing with bombs and landmines, hostage taking and targeted attacks upon civilians regarded as enemies.

Different women associations are fighting with the atrocities of the Armed Personnel with different Acts and Bills in the State of Manipur especially the Armed Forces Special Power Act. The world famous naked protest in front of the Assam Rifles Forces on July 2004 was a remarkable protest performed by the women of All Manipur Social Reformation and Development Samaj in connection with the merciless killing of Thangjam Manorama Devi of Imphal East District. Not only in group, Irom Chanu Sharmila is continuing her hunger strike against this brutal Act. For opening the deaf ear of the Government, on 10th December, 2008, under the leadership of Smt. K. Taruni Devi, President of the All Manipur Social Reformation and Development Samaj formed a group called 'Sharmila Kanba Lup' at PDA Complex Porompat. Their motto is to support Sharmila and demand to remove AFSPA from Manipur. A continuous relay hunger strike is still going on by the women from different parts of the State.[14] People, mainly women of all sections support this movement because the cases related with the violation of human rights is increasing so much, and Army and State forces commit the crime of human rights violation in the name of this Act.

Impact of Violence against Women

Gender-based violence encompasses a wide range of human rights violation, including sexual abuse of children, rape, domestic violence, sexual assault and harassment, trafficking of women and girls and several harmful traditional practices. Anyone of these abuses can leave deep psychological scars, damage the health of women and girls in general, including their reproductive and sexual health, and in some instances, result in death. Violence against women has been recognized as "the most pervasive yet least recognized human rights abuse in the world." Accordingly, the Vienna Human Rights Conference and the Fourth World Conference on Women gave priority to this issue which jeopardizes women's lives, bodies, psychological integrity and freedom. Violence against women and girls constitute the single most prevalent and universal violation of human rights. Human rights violation has served to fuel conflicts and act as a recruiting sergeant for militant groups in many parts of the country.[15] Arbitrary detention, torture, and the killing of peaceful critics have had the effect of closing democratic and peaceful paths of opposition, forcing organizations underground and fuelling a growth in militancy. Not only from the side of the state actor, many militant groups have been responsible for human rights abuses, including torture, indiscriminate killing with bombs and landmines, hostage taking and targeted attacks upon civilians regarded as enemies.

Violence against women exists in various forms in everyday life in all societies. There are several instances where rape victims in any society do not report the atrocity committed against them for fear of physical safety. This speaks poorly of both—which is deeply patriarchal in its attitudes and our law-enforcing machinery. Instead of enabling women who have been victims of sexual assault cope with their trauma, large sections of our society often heap indignity on them.

Armed conflict situations arise at the instance of external aggressive by a foreign country or internal strife within the country ranging from ethnic strife, communal hatred, attack on marginalized communities and minorities, religious fundamentalism, extremism, class and caste conflict and state repression in the event of armed conflict, the state military (the protector) serves many functions. According to conventional world politics wisdom, the military serves to protect the borders of states and the citizens within them from outside aggression. History of India depicts a good list of battles which decided the fate of a large number of Indian war heroes, who sacrifice their life for the sake of their motherland. Table 3.5 shows the martyrdoms who sacrificed their lives in different wars since Independence.

Table 3.5: Number of martyrdoms who sacrificed for the sake of their motherland

Sl. No.	Year	Name of the War	Number of martyrdoms
1.	1948	Jammu & Kashmir Operation	1104
2.	1962	China War	3250
3.	1965	Pakistan War	3264
4.	1971	Bangladesh Liberation War	3841
5.	1987	IPKF Operation in Sri Lanka	1157
6.	1999	Kargil War	522
Total		**Six wars**	**13138**

Source: Media information.

The military serves other less laudable functions such as protecting repressive state elites from rebellion by their own people. This situation is happened as the maintenance of the internal security of states at the expense of non-elite citizens. Many of the experiences of women and girls in armed conflict are similar to those of men and boys. They suffer the same trauma, are forcibly displaced, injured and killed and have difficulties in making a living during and after conflict. But there are differences between the two—the type of experiences got by the girls and women are not suffered by the boys and men at all in some cases. But all the problems suffered by men and boys are suffered by the women and girls altogether. Women and girls have became prime targets of armed conflict and suffered its impact disproportionately particularly as gender based and sexual violence have become weapons of warfare and one of the defining characteristics of contemporary armed conflicts. Women and children also constitute the majority of the world refugees and internally displaced persons. Women and girls are vulnerable to all forms of violence, but particularly sexual violence and exploitation including torture, rape, mass rape, forced pregnancy, sexual slavery, enforced protection and trafficking. Easy access to weapons in increased interpersonal violence including domestic violence, which often continues and may even increase in the aftermath of conflict. So, the Security Council Resolution, 1325 (2000), the Action Proposed by the Secretary

General—Recognized the extent of violation of the human rights of women and girls during armed conflict, and ensure that awareness of these violations is factor in planning and implementing all peace support operations.

Conclusion

There will be no peace without development, and there will be neither peace nor development without social justice. We can understand development as an integral process of social, economic and political transformation which implies the humanization of the living and working conditions for both sexes within this context, the promotion of the status and role of women in development. Such, development requires the maximum participation of women in all fields, not violent actions against them. So, when violations against women or girls are not recognized as human rights abuses, women are collectively diminished as human beings and denied part of their humanity. Human rights are not a gift granted at the pleasure of Governments nor can they be withheld by Governments, or applied to some people and not to others. When Governments act like this and deny human rights to a group of people in society, they must be held accountable. But Governments are not the only one's responsible for human Rights abuses against women. Corporation, NGOs, private individuals etc. should also be held accountable. Too often cultural relativism in the form of social and cultural tradition is used as an excuse to deny the human rights of women. But we need to take account this factor very seriously. The universality of human rights means that they apply equally to women as well as to men. This universality of rights—universality both in understanding and in application—is the most powerful tool against gender violence, intolerance, racism, xenophobia and terrorism. Violence whether justified in the name of communism, nationalism or democracy or glorified in the name of class struggle or *jihad,* destroys not only human lives, but even the very causes that are touted as justifications for their violence.

Notes

1. Tyagi, Suresh Kumar, 2012, *Human Rights and Democratization,* Swastic Publications, Delhi, p. 83.
2. Roy, Hiranmoy and Adhikari, Kingshuk, 2008, *Influence of Social Sector Expenditure on Human Development,* in Ray, Asok Kumar and Sengupta, Sutapa, (eds.) in *Population Dynamics in North-East India,* Om Publication, p. 335.
3. Sarkar, Anchal, (2006), *Gender and Development,* Pragun Publications, New Delhi, pp. 34-35.
4. *Times of India,* dt. 10-1-2009, p. 8.
5. *Amnesty International Report* 2007, p. 12.
6. *Women's Rights are Human Rights,* Amnesty International India, 2004.
7. Chauhan, Laxmidhar, 2007, *Women and the Law,* Mittal Publication, New Delhi, p. 38.
8. Th. Binarani Devi, 2008, Women's Movements in Conflict Situation of Manipur, in Ray, Asok Kumar and Chakraborty, Satyabrata (eds.) *Society, Politics and Development in North-East India,* Concept Publishing Company Pvt. Ltd., New Delhi, pp. 110-111.
9. Section 3 of the Domestic Violence Act, 2005.
10. *Amnesty International Report 2007,* p. 12.
11. *Times of India,* dt. 5-11-2011, p. 6.
12. Phukon, Dolly, 2008, New Economic Policy and Its Impact on Traditional Skills of Women in North-East India, in Day, B. Dutta, Dev Bimal J. (eds.) *Globalization and North-East India,* Concept Publishing Company Pvt. Ltd., New Delhi, p. 349.
13. *Getting Away With Murder,* Human Rights Watch, August 2008, p. 4.
14. *Interview* with Smt. K. Taruni Devi, President, All Manipur Social Reformation and Development Samaj.
15. *Human Development Report,* 2005, p. 51.

4
Politics and Women Empowerment

Women, by constituting an integral part of any society and culture, are often underestimated and discriminated in different forms and respects. Many a time, the contribution of women is neither given due attention nor marginalized while formulating socio-economic development plans. Being characterized by tradition of sex discrimination and social stratification, the Indian women also occupy a place of subordination to men in many occasions. In maximum societies, women had been considered naturally unsuited to political activity and had been formally or informally excluded from it. The legacy of this old belief, reinforced by unequal domestic division of labour not only handicaps women in the pursuit of political office, but also prevent them from being active in political participation of any type of nature. Being influenced by unique physical, racial and socio-cultural diversities quite different from the rest of the country, North-East India witnesses a great variation in socio-economic conditions of women in both spatial and social terms. Valley areas of Manipur, portions of Assam and some parts of Tripura are populated by Hindu communities and remaining is tribal in North-East India. Political analysts and historians are of the view that tribal societies are more liberal and there are not so serious cases of gender discrimination and differences. T.C. Hodson in his book, *'The Naga Tribes of Manipur'* mentioned that "I do not remember any case of cruelty to women and children in these tribes."[1] But when we examine and analyze the whole social condition in detail non-discrimination is prevalent only due to the sacrifice and relentless activities of the women in their respective societies. Women in the Kabui Naga Tribes of Manipur bear the overall responsibilities along the household works. The activities of women in these communities are described as "In the grey of the morning the females of the family are astir and the village resounds with the blows of the long pestle in the wooden mortar beating out the rice from the husk. This finished, breakfast is cooked both for the family and the pigs, for the latter the husk mixed with other refuse serves the purpose. Breakfast over, which its usually at about sunrise, the women proceed for water, which they fill into bamboo tubes and bring on their backs. Then they go for firewood, and this brought, they set about the internal economy of the house; that is, to see to their husband's drink being in proper quantity and quality, to their spinning or to their weaving, or any of the other household occupations except sweeping the house clean, an act in which they have no pride."[2] It is obvious that discrimination exists. Activities of the women are not counted. Their activities are considered as natural. Women do not have the opportunities that men do. And women that do not conform to the system, who try to break with the accepted patterns, are stigmatized as 'odds' and 'unfeminine'. But the status of women is key indicator to the progress of a society as well as of the country. They shares distinct and equal footsteps along with the men folk of the society. Women need protection of their rights and interests. Male alone should not make laws pertaining to the rights of women. Their active participation in law making is of vital importance as there are good reasons to believe that issues affecting women are not given adequate scope in public life.[3]

Women are the beginning of everything. On her side, she needs to understand everything, aware of all the consequences, be able to fight and challenge all those obstacles, to acquire all the knowledge in all-round her all the time. But without empowerment, the above mentioned conditions are impossible. That is why women empowerment is the most important step for the respective Governments. During the Indian freedom struggle, women's emancipation found one of the major thrusts of social reformers and included issues such as child marriage, the plight of widows, and education for women. These issues arose from the pivotal elements of the patriarchal system which measured the women's usefulness only in terms of her sexual and reproductive functions and dictated her inherently subservient role. The forces of orthodoxy staunchly defended the system, while the reformers attacked it although not necessarily in a united manner. The championship of these issues by reformers, in different parts of India, was both the result and cause of British government's policies of opening schools for girls as well as boys, and legislations, especially the laws to abolish the practice of *Sati* (1829), to legalize remarriage of upper caste widows (1856), and to raise the minimum age for girls at the consummation of marriage to twelve (1891). But one of the biggest responsibilities of the empowered women today is how to synthesize what has been valuable and timeless in our ancient traditions with what is good and valuable in modern thought. Now, for India to become what we want it to become with a modern, rational society and firmly based on what is good in our ancient tradition and in our soil, for this we have a thinking public, thinking young women who are not content to accept what comes from any part of the world but are willing to listen to it, to analyze it and to decide whether it is to be accepted or whether it is dethrone out and this is the sort of empowerment which we want, which enables our young people to adjust to this changing world and to be able to contribute to it.

Women are assets who can reshape and reconstruct the society in all aspects such as socially, economically, politically, academically and so on. So, women should be empowered with greater access to knowledge and resources, greater autonomy in decision-making to enable them to have greater ability to plan their lives or have greater control over the circumstances that influence their lives and free from shackles imposed on them by customs, beliefs and practices.

Women empowerment is a process of social transformation, and it is the ability to mobilize the women themselves around self-defined concerned and priorities. The concept of women empowerment is empowering women socially, economically and politically, so that, they can break away from male domination and claim equality with them. This concept was first introduced at Nairobi in 1985. It claimed women empowerment in terms of redistribution and utilization of social powers and control of resources in favour of women. The Director of UNIFEM on the occasion of the Fourth World Conference of Women in Beijing 1995 said that empowerment has four components:

(i) A women's sense of self-worth;
(ii) The right to determine choices;
(iii) The power to control their own lives within and outside the home; and
(iv) Their ability to influence the direction of social change and to create social and economic order nationally and internationally.[4]

Serious steps have been taken up at the national and international level with the beginning of 1980s in connection with the topic of women emancipation and empowerment. India committed itself to several congregation on women's issues like the most prominent being the UN sponsored Fourth World Conference on Women in Beijing in September 1995. It focused on key gender issues as (i) women's right to decide freely on matters related to their own 'sexuality'; (ii) prohibition of violence against women including rape in wartime, domestic abuse, genital mutilation, and sexual harassment in workplace; (iii) discrimination against female infants and girls; (iv) women's need for access to credit and other instruments of economic power; (v) the equal right of women to inherit; and (vi) the need to strengthen, protect, and support the family as the basic unit of the society.[5] United Nations declared 25th November as the "International Day for Elimination of Violence against Women." And, the year 2001 was declared as the "International Women's Empowerment Year" by the United Nations. Simultaneously, the Government of India also declared the same year as "Women Empowerment Year".

Empowerment does not mean competition with men; in fact empowering women will enable them to eradicate all kinds of ignorance. They can participate in all kinds of activities and cooperate with men to bring about or more sociably and natural environment, e.g. in the field of literacy, health, social, economic, political, public administration, legal, local, global environmental issues, industrial, science and technology etc. From this point, empowerment is an active, multidimensional process which should enable women to realize full identity and powers in all spheres of life. It would consists of greater access to knowledge and resources, greater autonomy in decision-making, greater ability to plan their lives, greater control over the circumstances that influence lives and free them by customs, beliefs and practices.[6]

Empowerment of women is essentially a broader concept heralding a shift from unjust to just, subservient to successful, passive to active womenhood. It refers to reversing gender base social, economic and political inequalities. It involves a complex interplay of various factors like physical, social, economic, political, psychological and attitudinal.

Constitutional Provision for Women in India

In India, women have the right to vote and can contest the election. Even women members were there in the Constituent Assembly of India. In political sphere, India's women in general and Hindu women in particular, stood in the forefront of every movement. Modern Indian women are objects of admiration by people of the rest of the world for the role they played in the country's public life. Women in India have not only reached the highest positions of power, and equal political and civil rights as men without having to fight for them, but they also have been increasingly joining the higher ranks of administration. When we start making a comparison between the role and status of women in modern India and in the other countries of the world, particularly in the matter of emancipation of women, we are struck with unexpected contrasts. The part that has been played by women in the freedom struggle and in the politics has been more important than that played by women in most other countries of the world. While their Western counterparts had to struggle to get political citizenship, Indian women won the franchise at the same time as men, i.e. at the time of the National Independence in 1947, along with favourable legislation in many other areas. In India, conscious of their political rights and influenced by Western democratic values, women worked actively to generate political consciousness among women during the early decades of the twentieth century in India. They took up the issue of voting rights for women with the Secretary of the State for India, Lord Edwin Montagu, who was in India to discuss the demands for political reforms during the British Imperialism. The South Borough Franchise Committee was initially campaign launched by women's organizations and the support given to them by the Indian National Congress and other political parties, it was finally left to the provincial legislatures to decide the matter. Madras was first province to grant women franchise in 1920 followed by Bombay in 1921. While in Britain, Emmeline Pankhurst founded the Women's Franchise League in 1903, with her daughter Christabel (1880-1958), the Women's Social and Political Union (WSPU). She fought for women to have the same political status as men. The motto of the Suffragettes was 'deeds, not words'. They fought a long historic struggle for their political equality. In June 1918, the British women over 30 won the right to vote. On 2 July, 1928, just three weeks after Emmeline Pankhurst's death, a law was passed allowing all women over the age of 21 to vote.[7]

The fifteen Lok Sabha election is a fine blend of women in India. Although the women's reservation bill proposing 33 per cent reservation for women in Parliament was not passed despite repeated attempts to table it. In the new Lok Sabha highest number of women MPs were ever elected. At 58, the 15th Lok Sabha has 13 more women MPs than the last House and nine more than the previous best of 49 in the 13th Lok Sabha. However, this is still low in comparison with Parliaments of the industrialized countries. For the first time in the electoral history of India in many years, we see the hope of youths, brimming with energy, guided by a clutch of experienced people of great maturity and sagacity. Some important young women Congress MPs who have successes in this 15th Lok Sabha are—Mandasaur's Meenakshi Natarajan (36), Nagaur's Jyoti Mirdha (36), Bhiwani Mahendragarh's Shruti Choudhri (33) and Malda North's Mausam Noor (28)—come from different States and united by their agenda for development. The youngest MP of the 15th Lok Sabha is Agatha Sangma, 28 years, a women MP from NCP of Meghalaya. Regarding the success of women MP in the 15th Lok Sabha, intellectuals and eminent writers gave different comments. India's first women IPS officer Kiran Bedi says things changed for the better when women enter a male dominated field. She said, "After I joined the police force, it got more sensitized. Now, there are many women cops and more focus on women policing, even setting-up of all-women *thanas*. Similarly, more women in Parliament will bring a different perspective to the House. Even in their respective constituencies, they will be sensitive about a different and a wider range of issues, and will tackle them with a new approach altogether." Author and political commentator Shobha De is cautious: "As an optimist, one would like to believe it is a positive change, but it is not always about the numbers. It is quality and commitment that count finally. I hope the new women parliamentarians focus on issues directly related to enhancing the lives of less privileged women in our country. A society is judged by the status of its women and unfortunately, our track record in this context has been dismal indeed."[8]

Politically, in India, the people under a parliamentary democratic Government enjoy liberty, equality and fraternity; there is no discrimination only on the ground of race, caste, sex etc. Constitutionally and legally, no barrier exists in women having equality with; the principle for equal pay for equal work has been long accepted by all employees in the country, special laws to protect women from most of the socially degrading customs have been enacted and enforced. To attain the national objectives which are enshrined in the Preamble, the Constitution guarantees certain fundamental rights and freedoms such as freedom of speech, protection of life, personal liberty and prohibition of discrimination or denial of equal protection. One specific provision in Article 15(3), which empowers the state to make "any special provision for women and children." This is in violation of the fundamental obligation of non-discrimination among citizen, *inter alia,* on the ground of sex. Consequently, this provision has enabled the State to make special provision for women, particularly in the field of labour legislation like the Factories Act, the Mines Act, Child Labour Prohibition (Regulation) Act and so forth. Different Articles, like Art. 16(1), Art. 16(2), Art. 39(a), Art. 39(d), Art. 39(e), Art. 42 etc. are dealt with equality and avoidance of discrimination. Plan provisions for development of women have been receiving attention of the Government of India right from the very First Five Year Plan (1951-56). The shift in the approach from 'welfare' to 'development' of women could take place only in the Sixth Plan (1980-85). Accordingly, the Sixth Plan adopted a multidisciplinary approach with a special thrust on the three core sectors of health, education and employment. The Ninth Plan (1997-2002) made two significant changes in the conceptual strategy of planning for women. Firstly, 'Empowerment of Women' became one of the nine primary objectives of the plan. To this effect, the approach of the Plan was to create an enabling environment where women could freely exercise their rights both within and outside home, as equal partner along with men. Secondly, the plan attempted 'Convergence of Existing Services' available in both women specific and women related sectors. With this aims, it directed both the Centre and the States to adopt a special strategy of 'Women Component Plan' (WCP) through which not less than 30 per cent of funds/benefits flow to women from all general development sectors. It also suggested that a special vigil be kept on the flow of the earmarked funds/benefits through an effective mechanism to ensure that the proposed strategy brings forth a holistic approach towards empowering women.[9]

In recent years, the empowerment of women has been recognized as the central issue in determining the status of women. Since Independence, the Government of India has made concerted efforts towards women empowerment by removing gender biases so that women enjoy equal status *vis-à-vis* men in the real sense as enshrined in the Constitution of India. Some of the major initiatives taken by the Government are:

- Child Marriage Restraint Act, 1976.
- Equal Remuneration Act, 1976.
- Dowry Prohibition Act, 1961.
- Immoral Traffic (Prevention) Act, 1986.
- Indecent Representation of Women (Prohibition) Act, 1986.
- Commission of Sati (Prevention) Act, 1987.
- Medical Termination of Pregnancy Act, 1971.
- Pre-Natal Diagnostic Techniques (Regulation and Prevention of Misuse) Act, 1992.
- 73rd and 74th Amendments in the Constitution to provide reservation of seats for Women in Panchayats and Municipalities.
- Right to Property Act, 2005.
- Domestic Violence Act.

Machinery at National Level

Set-up exclusive Department of Women and Child Development in 1985 and the following organizations:

- National Institute of Public Corporation and Child Development,
- Central Social Welfare Board,
- Rashtriya Mahila Kosh,
- National Commission for Women,
- The Standing Committee on 'Empowerment of Women' set-up by Parliament, and
- National Commission on Self-Employed Women and Women in the Informal Sector.

Programme Initiatives

Department of Women and Child Development: Indira Mahila Yojana (IMY), Hostels for Working Women, Short Stay Home for Women and Girls, Mahila Samriddhi Yojana (MSY), Gender Sensitization and Awareness Generation, Support to Training and Employment Programme for Women (STEP), Training-*cum*-Employment-*cum*-Production Centre, Balika Samriddhi Yojana.

Central Social Welfare Board: Condensed Courses of Education and Vocational Training, Socio-Economic Programme for Women, Crèches for Working/Ailing Mothers' Children, Family Counselling Centres.

National Commission for Women: A statutory body, set-up under a Central Act in 1992, the Commission strives to achieve equity, equality and justice; pursues gender justice through intervention in cases of violation of equality, denial of opportunities and deprivation of women's rights. It arranges counselling and assistance to women victims of atrocities and women in distress all over the country.

Policies Advocating Women's Concerns

- National Plan of Action for Women 1976,
- National Perspective Plan for Women (1988-2000),
- National Plan of Action for the Girl Child, (1991-2000),
- Shram Shakti Report of the National Commission on Self-Employed Women and Women in the Informal Sector,
- National Nutrition Policy, and
- National Policy for the Empowerment of Women (draft)—Plan of Action to Combat Trafficking and Commercial Sexual Exploitation of Women and Children.

Future Programme

- Adopting National Policy for the Empowerment of Women,

- Convergence of Women Development Frogramme at the Central and State Level,
- Setting up Office of the Commission for Women's Rights, and
- Setting up National Resource Centre for Women.

Actual Status of Women in India and North-East

It was only in the late 1970s, that women realized that they were winners of a 'hollow fortress' as the social structures had largely remained unchanged. They have got the right to contest election just with the Independence of India. Women were elected from the first Parliamentary Election of 1952. But the number of women in Governmental Ministerial level is not increased with a desirable amount. And those countries where women received the political rights later than India are increasing the number of women in Governmental Ministerial level higher than India. Table 4.1 shows comparative figure of Indian women in political decision-making power along with some developing countries.

Table 4.1: Women's Political Participation

Sl. No.	Year women received rights		Year first women elected (E) or appointed (A) to parliament	Women in Governmental ministerial level	MDG Seats in Parliament held by women (% of total)			HDI rank
	To vote	To stand for election			Lower or single house		Upper house senate 2005	
					1990	2005		
Botswana	1965	1965	1979E	26.7	5	11.1	—	131
Uganda	1962	1962	1962A	23.4	12	23.9	—	144
Namibia	1989	1989	1989E	19.0	7	25.0	26.9	125
Gabon	1956	1956	1961E	11.8	13	9.2	15.4	123
India	1950	1950	1952E	8.4	5	8.3	11.6	177

Source: Human Development Report 2005.

The issues of women empowerment arises because of the stark reality that women are still marginalized and sidelined from the mainstream as a use and throw commodity. The patriarchal canopy had always denied women the warm rays of autonomy and freedom. The indeclinable gender bias has disfigured the face of humanity. This discrimination originates well before the birth of a girl and is sustained right through her womenhood. India is a nation whose nationhood is equated with the 'Mother India'; image the '*Bharat Mata*'. India is also a country having agricultural economy, where land is the main source sustenance, is connotatively associated with women in the form of '*Bhumi Devi*'. It is quite ironical that in spite of these symbolical attributions, women in India are viewed as 'second sex'.[10] Barbaric and savagist practices still continue to haunt women in the form of female foeticide, female infanticide, child labour, child marriage, dowry, rape, sexual harassment, gender inequality, molestation, eve teasing, forced prostitution, child pornography etc. The increasing number of early widowhood is in an alarming stage in this armed conflict region (between state and non-state actors and again between the non-state and non-state actors), as well as the area of golden triangle where the number of HIV/AIDS is in a remarkable stage. In our contemporary industrial society women are much deprived, defected and dominated by men.

The World Economic Forum (WEF) in its sixth annual report of the Global Gender Gap Index has ranked India 113 out of 135, with a score of 0.619. In 2010 India has ranked at 112, and in 2006 it was at position 98. Coming together with the UNDP Human Development Report and its statistics on India's low position on 129 out of 177 nations in the Gender Inequality Index, the WEF grading of India is not surprising, but is of concern. India ranks lowest on gender parity among the BRICS (Brazil, Russia, India, China, and South Africa) countries, whereas South Africa tops at position 14. Though Indian women received the right to vote during the British colonialism and 1950, after Independent, there is an enormous gender gap, and it has been overtaken by most nations. Switzerland, where women could vote from 1971, is now at 10th position, with four out of seven women cabinet ministers. Though India has successful women CEO and entrepreneurs, the WEF lists it at 123 in the field of legislators, senior officials and managers. In political empowerment India is up at rank 19 out of 135, however, it is down at position 98 when it comes to women in Parliament, and 87 to women in ministerial position.[11]

Women in North-East India play very important role in the social life. A study on social life and social change of North-East India would be incomplete without a study on women. Women participate in multifarious socio-economic activities, women who are facing a number of problems in the socio-economic spheres often form different organizations. But they face all the problems created by customs, cultures, and religions of their respective societies. During the freedom struggle, many women participated and they became Prime Minister, Chief Ministers, Governors and other dignitaries without taking the privilege of reservations at the national level. The courage and contribution of the women of Manipur in the famous Nupilan (women's war) of 1904 and 1939, Rani Gaidinliu led movement, and many other women led movements in the north-east could make a place for them in the history.[12] In the specific case of the north-eastern states where hundreds of tribes are busy to assert their respective strength by number the tasks of enhancing the status of women are very largely compromised with the call of primitive force for the survival of racial identity. Ironically, this is not confined to the tribal ethnic groups such as the Hindus, Muslims and the Christians where successions and religious rites are performed in proverbial and almost providential times.[13] Theoretically, women in North-East India enjoy a high social status because their societies are egalitarian. Although, the status of women is said to be highest but men in their societies do not treat the women as their equal. The customary laws of the various tribes in this region are in favour of men who continue to be superiority *vis-à-vis* women in their respective societies. With the implementation of 73rd Amendment Act, 1992 there is a scope for more democratic governance through decentralization of structure and powers and responsibilities to the self-governing bodies and through involving the people in shaping their own destiny. The Act is to bring far reaching changes towards the realization of the dream of power to the people. But the states of Nagaland, Mizoram, and Meghalaya remain out of the orbit of the 73rd

Amendment Act and the hill areas of Manipur, the District council minus the Sixth Scheduled provisions was once there, also do not came under the purview of the 73rd Amendment Act.[14] The Government might have reserved 33 per cent of the *panchayat* seats for women but in backward and remote villages the reservation is just for namesake. In many of the women reserved *panchayats,* husbands or any other male members of the family in this minority dominated locality who actually run the everyday affairs on behalf of their wives or any women relatives. Even though political parties are ambitious about empowerment of women in the state, women rights activists take it with skepticism. They said mere reservation of seats in local bodies or increasing quota for women's participation in state level politics does not mean empowerment. Reservation of seats is not real empowerment. Visibility of women in politics might have increased, but empowerment has not come yet. It is true in the *panchayats,* too, where women were just acting as rubber stamp of husbands. Until women become an intrinsic part of the decision-making process, we cannot call it empowerment merely by reserving seats for women.

When it comes to elections, nominations are made on the basis on winning ability of a candidate, and usually women are left behind. Regarding women's politico-electoral practices, Mahesh Rangarajan said, "Very few women in India own properties, few are highly educated and most of them do not wield much power. Electoral politics is about power and a section of society has been deprived of power completely. It should not be a surprise if they are missing from politics." According to him, "Politics being are of the most male dominated fields, women, even though they play the important role as voters; fail to rise up to governing position."

Due to the paternalistic family and male dominated political structures which do not provide space for women in decision-making bodies, women constituted 3.1 per cent of the total contestants in the 1996 election and did not occupy more than 6-10 per cent of the total seats in the State Legislative Assemblies and Parliament. In Manipur only six women have been elected in the State Legislative Assembly. Only one woman

M.P. was elected so far (Kim Gangte). Women's participation in local level political institutions like village *panchayats* and municipal bodies has also remained insignificant in spite of the Government's policy of cooption and reservation of seats for women.

It is generally believed that the responsibility of establishing social, economic and political justice/equality lies in the State. The Indian States, however, have failed to take adequate measures in emancipating and empowering women mainly because most individuals and/or political parties who control various organs of the State are intoxicated with patriarchal values. Moreover, in the contemporary era of liberalization, privatization and disinvestments, the State has abandoned the policy of welfare. Under these circumstances, empowerment of women is possible through voluntary action at the grassroots level. This is today the basic solution of women's problems throughout the country including the North-East.[15]

In North-East India, the most important problem of the present day society is women become the worst victim in case of insurgency and counter-insurgency situations. As a matter of fact, the position of women is just in a puzzle situation. They are very active in social life, running different types of economic activities, but they are not in decision-making. They organized different movements, giving pressure to the Government, and Non-governmental organizations too. Their way of agitationist movement is quite typical in certain occasions. But, they are not available or hardly available in the position of leadership in general. Women are abused, battered, molested, raped, murdered or forced to commit suicide. Protection for the victim and punishment for the guilty etc. are hard to come by. In this present day socio-political context, problems and issues in connection with human rights on women is increasing day-by-day. Women are becoming so active in the movements against the violence of human rights in general. Maximum front pages of the daily local papers are witnessing with the crimes related with fake encounter, extra-judicial killings etc. The rate of child trafficking illegally outside the State is on the rise. There have been no let up in triggering fake encounter, custodial killings and gross violation of human rights perpetrated by the security forces. Irom Sharmila Chanu has been fasting against the Armed Forces Special Power Act for the last more than eleven years. The social norms and customary laws of the different societies in this region are in favour of men who discriminate against women in their respective societies. These pose challenge to the women community in this region. There are millions of women who silently suffer injustice, violence, abuse, exploitation just because they are born as women. There are millions of young girls who languish as they do not have the key to open the door of opportunities for progress.

The customary laws of the various tribes of the region are always in favour of men. In the traditional society of Garo, women are ridiculed with a proverb "as a goat without teeth, a women lacks brain." "Nishis of Arunachal Pradesh possess wives as many as mithuns they have." The different Nagas believe that males possess six kinds of strength, females have only five and that is why, they christened boys on the sixth day after birth and girls on the fifth day. Moyon Nagas of Manipur considers that women have no permanent clan. After marriage husband's clan is imposed on them. Pre-marital clan identity is not valid. The Zeliangrong Nagas have a taboo that man is not to sleep with or touch her inner garments before going to war or for hunting. It is an omen of bad luck. On the other hand, Zemi Nagas do not eat the meat of an animal killed by women.[16] Simply Manipuri Meiteis are saying that "How many sins have committed before birth that a woman can make?" It is sometimes argued that women are not allowed to participate in certain spheres of life. In no religious practices, whether Hinduism, Islam or Christianity, women are allowed to act as a priest. The religion has been the spiritual need of the individual and the society. The system of priesthood evolved as a hereditary right of those born in priest family, and thus, has continued to exist till today. It is a faith of dependency which has allowed this practice to exist. The Hindus depend upon *Purohits* in Temples, the Christians depend upon *Padaris* in Churches, the Mohammedans depend upon *Mullahs* in Mosque, the Sikhs depend upon *Granthis* in Gurdwaras, and so in each religion and sect we find the prominent existence of priest. The dictates of different religions has reduced the women to second class surrogate entity in the society. In Hindu, Muslim and Christian societies the women are treated as merely perpetrators of human race. In the Hindu system, the *Upanishad-Vedanta* version has yielded place to Manu's Code of Life which relegated women to the lower hierarchy and considered as helpers on the path of *Moksha*. In the Muslim system, women are relegated to the status of procreators of the human race. The entire social and material relations are governed by this concept.[17] Christian mission contributed a lot to the educational development of the hilly people in North-East India. But, while men folk in India had been in contact with the ruling foreigners since the mid-eighteenth century, Indian women remained cut off from Western influence by traditional prejudices against female education and the custom of secluded women in the *zenana* (*harem*). Clearly, the Christian faith and Christian attitudes and habits (actually Western attitudes and habits) could never be firmly established in India until the women had been touched. Resistance to female education had been strong until the Mutiny of 1857-58; after that the elites were increasingly interested in having their women folk learn about the West. It was at this time that missionary women, appointed by Ladies' Missionary Societies, went out to of India with the expressed purpose of converting 'pure heathens', i.e. Indian women confined in the *zenanas*.[18] But there is certain exceptions in case of Manipuri Society. The case of Meitei women in performing religious rites and rituals in certain areas, even though that is not in all the areas, present a different picture no doubt. The traditional priestesses of Manipuri Society are called the '*Amaibi*'. They must be consulted for advice and *puja* on various matters. The *Amaibis* play a vital role in performance of rituals in temples and in the society. However, after the spread of Hinduism in Manipur the class of *Purohit* and *Pandits* has also emerged. No doubt, the Amaibism is related to the traditional Manipuri faith which is still practicing and Purohitism to the modern Hinduism.[19]

The problem of 'honour killings' needs attention of all concerned. The issue is linked to gender equality and women empowerment, which is one of the goals included in the 'Millennium Development Goals' in the International Conference of 191 countries in the year 2000. Honour killing is becoming a serious issue in connection with the violation of women's human rights throughout the globe. This is the right time to fight against honour killing, if not it will be too late. It was a time in Manipur, women were respected, honoured and dignified their value at home, workplaces or where not. But now-a-days, front pages of the daily local papers are heading with crimes against women; including cases of honour killings like women commit suicide. But, something or many things behind the cases—may be due to dowry; not having baby boy etc. All cases of honour killings must be properly and effectively registered, investigated and prosecuted and the perpetrators punished. States must ensure that adequate civil remedies and compensatory provisions exist for victims. Particularly, States should through education and information campaigns ensure that police officials, prosecutors and judiciary have appropriate awareness and knowledge of the problem of honour killings including the cases of and cultural considerations relating to honour killings, the legislation relevant to these crimes. If such campaigns are not carried out it can hardly be expected that the police investigations or prosecution of honour killings will be effective; let alone that the police has the capacity to provide protection to a woman at the risk of honour killing.[20]

There still exists a wide gap between the goals enunciated in the Constitution, legislation, policies, plans, programmes and related mechanisms on the one hand and the situational reality of the status of women in India, on the other. This has been analyzed extensively in the Report of the Committee on the Status of Women in India: "Towards Equality," 1974 and highlighted in the National Perspective Plan for Women, 1988-2000, the Shramshakti Report, 1988 and the "Platform for Action, Five Years After—An Assessment".[21] Gender stereotyping and violence at the domestic and social levels are some of the ongoing manifestations. The main causes of gender inequality are related to social and economic structure, which is based on informal and formal norms and practices. Consequently, the access of women, particularly those belonging to weaker sections including Scheduled Castes/Scheduled Tribes/Other Backward Classes and minorities, majority of whom are in the rural areas and in the informal, unorganized sector—to education, health and productive resources, among others, is inadequate. There they remain largely marginalized, poor and socially excluded.[22]

Traditionally, assigned gender roles circumscribe women's choices in education and careers and compel women to assume the burden for household responsibilities. Initiatives and programmes aimed at women's increased participation in decision-making are hindered by a lack of human and financial resources for training and advocacy for political career and accountability of elected officials for promoting gender equality and women's participation in public life. Despite vigorous campaigning by women's groups and despite the States commitment to increasing women's political participation, all political parties have been more than reluctant to file women candidates.

Ideals are also changing with the constitutional guarantee of different opportunities to the women in every sphere of life. Career is the symbol of new aspirations of women. Professionally, they are becoming doctors, engineers, teachers, lawyers etc. Liberal political thinking, urbanization, Westernization and industrialization have hardened the perception and experiences of women. But structural constraints are felt in the preference of their family roles that are often conflicting with their professional lives. The working women experience a great deal of pressure both at home and in society. The family expectations demand a traditional feminine role. Therefore, though women have progressive attitude and wider outlook most of them loose interest due to the conservative pressure put by the in-laws and husbands.

Although the policies and programmes of the Government seem to be quite useful and effective on papers, the Government must take necessary steps to implement these policies at the grassroots levels. The implementing authorities or officials are to be made accountable for every action they take. Because, in spite of all the efforts made by the political decision-makers, the long established beliefs and notions about female inferiority and the social prescription and prohibitions build around them have proved a hard nut to crack and as a result, women find it difficult to use the existing facilities to remove the hindrances of equality. Arguments for women seat reservation in the Parliament as well as in the State Legislative Assemblies are also raised from different quarters. A Bill on women reservation of seat is also lying in the Parliament. But a consensus decision on this Bill is yet residual and the Bill has not yet been passed in the Parliament due to lack of commitment and political will. Political reservations and provision of jobs for some middle class women are not sound methods for empowering women. Question of legal rights with regard to inheritance, divorce, title (*patta*) to land were raised by women in discussion groups and public meetings as well as in the courts. In North-East India, mainly in the tribal societies even after the introduction of Right to Property Act, 2005, women do not have land ownership, but they are engaged in cultivation, doing all the pre-harvest and post-harvest works. We, therefore, find that in the turn of new millennium women's position in different walks of life would remain at the low level. In agriculture, women are workers giving only their labour, but they have no decision-making power in various activities. The decision-making power of women is limited since, they do not have earning power. Even where they are earner, their decision-making power in the household are compromised and curtailed as their outside activities are limited. This is the general feature of women's status in the country. The rhetoric of empowerment is enabling women to become victims of oppressors who should be brought to book. Our judges and lawyers, the police and the criminal justice system in most of the cases fail to give justice to women victims, and the offenders are acquitted most of the time. Policy and its implementation have made many prescriptions in different directions. Many new responsibilities have been added without any reduction in the basic set of deprivations of work burdens; employment and education are becoming tools for family welfare. Ideally, these should have been women's source of freedom; birth control is manipulating for population control rather than relieving women from reproductive burdens. Health issues which came to the fore, particularly in relation to population control programmes sponsored by Governments or by international agencies included dangers inherent in the use and misuse of newly developed contraceptive devices; lack of adequate maternal and childcare facilities; need for attention to illness specific to women such as menstrual pain and post-partum backache. The possibilities opened by the procedure of amniocentesis to determining the sex of a foetus in the early weeks of pregnancy give rise to widespread abortion of girl child and to a heated debate on the ethical issue involved.

Conclusion

Serious attention and a fresh look are required to reorient our developmental model and policies, so that, economic development and women's development do not work as cross-purposes. A concerted attempt has to be made to evolve strategies for the economic independence and socio-political empowerment of the majority of the poor, and illiterate women in India, in general and North-East India in particular. Political empowerment of women is only a part of the overall mainstreaming of women. At the political level only microscopic minority of women at the helm of affairs, can affect the change in the life of women. Since, women are considered the most oppressed section of the society, the term 'women empowerment' has come to be associated with women struggle for social justice.

The political equality guaranteed by the democratic constitutions in the form of fundamental rights, political rights etc. is not able to penetrate deeply in the social roots in spite of many policies and programmes of the Government. The democratic government has also a great responsibility to create favourable socio-economic and political atmosphere for the empowerment of women, making them capable citizens of the State to discharge their duties in a positive and rightful manner. Women who were subjected to various kinds of subordination and inferiority position due to traditional social norms, beliefs and practices, handed down from generation to generation depicting gender roles are called for to empower themselves from within and from the laws, enactments, policies framed by the Government. Democracy promised them the enjoyment of equal political rights with men as candidates as well as voters in the electoral process and equal participation in the decision-making process of the State. But, in all democratic countries of the world, women participating in the decision-making process are found to be less than men. The question is how this happens after so many covenants, conventions, passed by the United Nations making women equal with men in their respective constitutions. There still exists a big gap between what is written in the Constitution and various laws passed by the Governments and what is prevailing in practice. In connection with the solution of the problems of crimes against women, changes needed in society's values more than the legal changes. However, the task is not very easy. It is not enough to offer *sarees* or *mangalsutras* to their daughters and sisters, but it is time how to buy *saree* or *mangalsutra*. These tokens build on rather than challenges, the customary notion of womenhood in India. It is facile to promise safety and security through better policing and tougher laws, locating the source of women's insecurity in the sphere of law enforcement. This is likely to satisfy some men who are concerned about women's safety, but not women, who instinctively know that the male violence that stalks them into every corner of their life is beyond the physical grasp of even that rare bird, the good cup etc.

Women empowerment has various dimensions and only change of law is not enough to bring about change in real condition. In the spheres of social and household relations the important task is to raise the social awareness by continuous exhortation. Every person in the society and in the family has to be aware of the rights, needs, well and woes, pleasure and pain as well as honour and dignity of the women. When women became the decision-makers or at the managerial position, they would be able to break the glass ceiling around them and to create women friendly environment. Women in such position would also help to bring about change in attitude, beliefs and thoughts and in enhancing motivation and self-confidence among them. As the wearer knows where the shoe pinches clearly, women acknowledged their problems very clearly. So, women have to organize themselves to assert their rights and extract their rights. Decentralized democratic administration is the most useful mechanism to empower women. We need to understand the real meaning of decentralized democracy which gives the real taste of political participation to all the people directly. Society will have to understand that issues of the women should not be treated as the issues and problems of the women alone, it should be treated as the issues and problems of the whole society. In the social life the bias against women and girl child has to be fought by social movements and by ensuring freedom to women from the oppressive social codes. Both men and women will have to work together in this direction, so that human resources are not wasted or exploited by the brutal forces.

Notes

1. Hodson, T.C., 2007, *The Naga Tribes of Manipur,* Low Price Publications, New Delhi, p. 7.
2. *Ibid.,* pp. 39-40.
3. Borah, Anjan Jyoti, 2008, Literacy, Education and Political Participation of Women in Meghalaya: With Special Reference to Garo Hills—A Study, in Gassah, L.S. (ed.), *Women Empowerment Movement in North-East India,* Omson Publication, New Delhi, p. 124.
4. Bordoloi, Ritimoni, 2008, Empowerment, Education and Social Development of Women of Asom, in Ray, B. Dutta and Ray, Asok Kumar (eds.) *Women Emancipation, Focus North-East India,* Om Publication, New Delhi, p. 183.
5. Ghose, Chitra; Ray, Soma and Chande, Chandni, 2002, *Opening the Closed Window,* Progressive Publishers, Kolkata, p. 83.
6. A. Henia, 2008, Education and Women Empowerment in Gassah, L.S. (ed.), *Women Empowerment Movement in North-East India,* Omson Publication, New Delhi, p. 81.

7. Norwegian Centre for Human Rights, University of Oslo, Human Killing needs Attention, Ray, Vikas Narayan, (ed.) *Larkiyon ka Inkilab Jindabad,* Sahitya Upakrama, Etihashbad Prakashan, Allahabad, 8th Edition, September 2009, p. 71.
8. *Times of India,* dt. 26-5-2009, p. 5.
9. Sankaran, Kamla, 2006, Women, Work and Empowerment, in Anjali Gandhi (ed.), *Women's Work Health and Empowerment,* Aakar Books, Delhi, pp. 23-24.
10. Bhowmik, Krishna, 2006, *Indian Women, the Ushering of a New Dawn,* Mittal Publication, New Delhi, p. 68.
11. *Times of India,* 5-11-2011, p. 6.
12. Th. Binarani Devi, 2008, Women Emancipation: A Way for Removing Gender Discrimination, in Ray B. Dutta and Ray, Asok Kumar (eds.) *Women Emancipation, Focus North-East India,* Om Publication, New Delhi, p. 325.
13. Banerjee, Amalesh, 2006, Women Empowerment and Development, in Ray, B. Dutta and Ray, Asok Kumar (ed.), *Dynamics of Power Relations in Tribal Societies of North-East India,* Om Publication, New Delhi, p. 1127.
14. Th. Binarani Devi, 2006, Position, Power and Functions of Women in Kuki Society, in Ray, B. Dutta and Ray, Asok Kumar (eds.), *Dynamics of Power Relations in Tribal Societies of North-East India,* Om Publication, New Delhi, p. 199.
15. Chattopadhyay, Tapan Kumar, 2008, Voluntary Action and Women Emancipation, in Ray, B. Dutta and Ray, Asok Kumar (eds.) *Women Emancipation, Focus North-East India,* Om Publication, New Delhi, p. 325.
16. Saharia, Umesh Ch. and Bhattacharjee, 2008, Crime Against Women, A Problem of Female Emancipation, in Ray, B. Dutta and Ray, Asok Kumar (eds.) *Women Emancipation, Focus North-East India,* Om Publication, New Delhi, p. 112.
17. Banerjee, Amalesh, *op. cit.,* p. 257.
18. Forbs, H. Geraldine, 2000, In Search of the 'Pure Heathen'—Missionary Women in Nineteenth Century India, in Thorner, Alice and Krishnaraj (eds.) *Ideals, Images and Real Lives,* Sameeksha Trust, Hyderabad, p. 68.
19. Th. Binarani Devi, 2011, *Women's Movement in Manipur,* Concept Publishing Company Pvt. Ltd., New Delhi, p. 76.
20. Norwegian Centre for Human Rights, University of Oslo, Human Killing needs Attention, Ray, Vikas Narayan, (ed.) *Larkiyon ka Inkilab Jindabad,* Sahitya Upakrama, Etihashbad Prakashan, Allahabad, 8th Edition, September 2009, p. 70.
21. Singh, K.K., 2006, Women Empowerment in Relation to the National Policy for the Empowerment of Women, in Anjali Gandhi (ed.), *Women's Work Health and Empowerment,* Aakar Books, Delhi, p. 26.
22. *Ibid.,* p. 27.

5

Electoral Politics and Women

A successful democracy requires a participant society in which power is shared and authoritative decisions are made by representatives of all the people in that society. A democratic government aims at justice and happiness. Justice because no man or class or group will be strong enough to wrong others; happiness because each man judging best what is good for him, will have every chance of pursuing it. The principles of liberty and equality are justified by the result they yield. It is a government not run by any particular individual or a class, but by elected representatives of the people. Simply, power is vested in the people, and the people should be allowed to choose their leaders. In the words of W.F. Willoughby—in a popular government of representative type, the electoral branch may be viewed as the foundation upon which the whole structure of government is erected. It is true logical that a consideration of the several branches of government should begin with it. Democracy, as a matter of principle, does not differentiate between men and women. For a democratic government there must be a democratic society. Modern democratic models did not develop theoretically in most of the Third World countries. Both on logical and rational grounds political rights cannot be denied to any section of people. The right of voting is based upon moral and rational grounds rather than on physical considerations. Indian democracy too, unfortunately, lacks the effective participation of all its citizens. Under representation of women in political institutions is seen as a by-product of gendered spaces and opportunity structures. Their participation is seen not only as control to the functioning of democracy, but also for women's ability to struggle for their rights and challenge the ideologies and hierarchies which keep them subordinated. The structure of political life for the ordinary women has largely remained hidden in the private sphere. Many feminists feel that democracy has failed to recognize women as political citizens in its theory and practice, and it has been more rewarding towards men than women. Man had all through the ages, dominated womenhood, subjected their women to inhuman treatment and deprived them of their just rights and privileges. They could defend themselves against unjust class legislation only if they had the right to vote and their views got adequate representations. In fact, the admission of women in politics would introduce in political life a purifying, ennobling and refining influence that not only would tend to elevate the tone of public life and bring about more wholesome political conditions in society, but also would ensure better government. To deny her right to suffrage was to deprive womenhood of the instinct of good citizenship. Women were the cradle of civilization and the future of every state depended upon her active participation in the affairs of government. If she was deprived of the civic sense, she had nothing to impart to her children. Finally, women enjoyed all civil rights, it was inconsistent and irrational not give them political rights. Political rights must necessarily go with civil rights.

One important issue that challenges the existing romanticized understanding of empowered Manipuri women comes from the fact that women continue to be either silenced or deprived in terms of political representation. While historical legacies promise a fertile environment for women's participation in the modern representative form of politics, women's role is negligible other than exercising their periodic franchise. Present prevailing patriarchal social structure do not encourage women to be active in electoral politics. Constitutionally and legally, no barrier exists in women having equality with men; special laws to protect women from most of the socially degrading customs have been enacted and enforced. In spite of all these, the long established belief and notion about female inferiority and social prescription and prohibitions built around them have proved a hard nut to crack and as a result, women find it difficult to use the existing facilities to remove the hindrances of equality.

Social Factors and Electoral Behaviour

Due to the paternalistic family and male dominated political structures which do not provide space for women in decision-making bodies. Politics is essentially an art of acquiring and co exercising power—the power to effectively influence the decision-making processes and policies and implementing desired changes. With a strict patriarchal psyche, decisions are meant to be taken by men and followed by women. They are expected to tow the line made by men. Qualities such as rationality, self-discipline, competition, universality are considered to be important for political participation, which are considered to be in abundance in the males. On the contrary, women are associated with qualities like docile, submissiveness, protected etc. This gender stereotype leads to the marginalization of women in the political arena as they are advised to keep away from politics and play only feminine and non-competitive roles. Indian culture assigns the women the responsibility of primarily parenting and nurturing—accordingly, developed a psychological make-up and choose the role of 'care giver' and prefer to confine them to the private sphere, i.e. home. The women who are keen on pursuing a career in politics enter the political sphere at a later age when they have fulfilled their responsibilities towards the family. However, this creates a greater problem for them as they have to devote more energy and struggle hard in order to compete with the men who have made an early start. Those who opposed women's suffrage emphasized that women was the ministering angel of home and maternity was her proper mission. The exaction of political life is inconsistent with the duties of child bearing and the rearing of families. Nature had not intended her for political life. Her participation in politics was sure to destroy the integrity of the home. If husband and wife differed in political views and supported opposing candidates, it might mean discord in family life. Moreover, women would loss respect and honour which was naturally due to them, if they got themselves involved in the mud and mire of political controversies. Their participation in public affairs, in brief, would destroy their qualities as mothers and home-makers. The opponents of women suffrage further pointed out that women had shown general apathy in public affairs wherever they were granted franchise. They were unable, being physically weaker, to perform the arduous duties of citizenship and, as such, they had no right to demand the privilege of franchise. Besides, women would be guided by emotion rather than by reason in electing the representatives. And, finally, their interest in public affairs would last only until the novelty wore off.[1]

At the beginning, during the British period in India, conscious of their political rights and influenced by Western democratic values, women worked actively to generate political consciousness among women during the early decades of the twentieth century in India. They took up the issue of voting rights for women with the Secretary of the State for India, Lord Edwin Montagu, who was in India to discuss the demands for political reforms during the British Imperialism. The South Borough Franchise Committee was initially campaign launched by women's organizations and the support given to them by the Indian National Congress and other political parties it was finally left to the provincial legislature to decide the matter. Madras was first province to grant women franchise in 1920 followed by Bombay in 1921.

For the first time in the electoral history of India in many years, we see the hope of youth, brimming with energy, guided by a clutch of experienced people of great maturity and sagacity. Some important young women Congress MPs who have successes in the 15th Lok Sabha are—Mandasaur's Meenakshi Natarajan (36), Nagaur's Jyoti Mirdha (36), Bhiwani Mahendragarh's Shruti Choudhri (33) and Malda North's Mausam Noor (28)—come from different states and united by their agenda for development. The youngest MP of the 15th Lok Sabha is Agatha Sangma, 28 years, a woman MP from NCP of Meghalaya. Regarding the success of women MP in the 15th Lok Sabha, intellectuals and eminent writers gave different comments. After September 2013 certain changes exhibited in the size of women members in the Parliament of different countries of the world. Rwanda, first time ever that women account for more than 60 per cent of MPs in a Parliament anywhere, i.e. 63.8 per cent of the total MP are women, Nepal has 30 per cent (33rd rank), China has 25 per cent (61th rank), Pakistan has 19.5 per cent (72nd rank), Bangladesh has 20 per cent (74th rank), India has only 10.9 per cent (111th rank), another South Asian country which is below India is Sri Lanka, which has only 5.8 per cent (133th rank).

Women's participation in local level political institutions like village *panchayats* and municipal bodies has also remained insignificant in spite of the Government's policy of cooption and reservation of seats for women. It is generally believed that the responsibility of establishing social, economic and political justice/equality lies in the State. The Indian States, however, have failed to take adequate measures in emancipating and empowering women mainly because most individuals and/or political parties who control various organs of the State are intoxicated with patriarchal values. Moreover, in the contemporary era of liberalization, privatization and disinvestments, the State has abandoned the policy of welfare. Under these circumstances, empowerment of women is possible through voluntary action at the grassroots level. This is today the basic solution of women's problems throughout the country including the North-East.[2] It is true that traditionally, the Meitei women's political status as such and the scope for their formally taking part in the decision-making process and in the affairs of the Government as well as their rights in sharing the inheriting property did not commensurate with the vital role played by them in economic and cultural sphere. It was an eye opener with the few words of Rahul Gandhi, Vice President, AICC, during the election rally at Tumkur in Karnataka on Sunday, the 16th February, 2014, "India cannot be a superpower until we empower women. Wherever women are being empowered and given a chance, those States are progressing rapidly."[3] There may be politics of winning electoral sympathy from the public or some may even criticize as political gimmick of election times, but what the statement shows is the value and credit of women as an integral part to the national growth and development. Besides, significant role that women performs in a democratic political process of any country, which is true mainly in a developing country like India. It is a socially well accepted reality in most Indian households, even where both spouses are working, that women end up handling most household chores. With the report of the survey conducted by Organization for Economic Cooperation and Development, Indian women spent a huge 298 minutes on routine housework such as cooking, laundry, pets and home maintenance. They spend 221 minutes on leisure which includes watching TV, sports and entertaining, compared to 283 minutes for men. Again, Indian men spend more than 670 minutes (11 hrs a day) on personal care—mostly sleeping, eating and drinking. Consequently, women are comparatively lack in the knowledge of the socio-political development of the country. While the male members considered it as the poor knowledge of women; and not considered about their discriminatory attitude towards women.

Political Parties and Election

An election is a formal decision-making process by which people choose an individual to hold public office. Election has been the usual mechanism by which modern representative democracy has operated. In such country, political system works through political parties. In a democratic country, political parties have raised extra legal or extra Constitutional bodies to fulfil the political aims of various types of individuals in the state. Political parties are developed because the Constitution provides for free elections, and it is a means for presenting alternative policies and candidates to the public for public approval. While openness and accountability are usually considered cornerstone of a democratic system, the act of casting a vote and contesting the election are usually an important stage. The political parties and groups make use of different variables for winning the battle of the ballot box. The political parties and groups make use of different variables for the sake of winning the battle of the ballot box. Despite making their profession for enlightened secularism, politicians can be found making appeals to the religious and communal sentiments of the people. They can also be found involved in exploiting the factors of language or money to achieve the purpose of emerging successful in the war of votes. Appeals are issued and canvassing campaigns conducted in the name of a particular policy or ideology for the same purpose. The interest of the voters and accordingly their behaviour at the time of voting is also influenced by the nature or purpose of the elections or the extent of the suffrage.[4] Even before Independence of India, with the organization of political parties, the male leaders have their different *attitude* towards the political participation of women in the structural development of political parties, even though active women who have keen interest in the socio-political development of the society. At the time of the Second National Congress at Bombay in 1889, Bradlaugh had suggested to Pandita Ramabai and other leading women that women delegates should be inducted from the beginning, so that, women's participation would be automatically ensured when the Congress developed the India's Parliament in future. Ranade and others did not encourage women's participation, but Ramabai, through great effort collected seven or eight women delegates.[5]

After Independent, the Constitution of India mentions very clearly about the equality and liberty for all the people without any condition of class, caste and sex. The numbers of women voluntary organizations are also increasing day-by-day. Women members in the political parties are also increasing. And periodic elections for the Indian Parliament and the State Legislatures have started since 1952. A gender gap is witnessed in contestation among the candidates during the elections. Political parties have always been reluctant to give tickets to women. They prefer to give tickets to the male candidates.[6] While the different political parties are talking about their support to the Women Reservation

Bill in the Parliament, the number of women candidates who have been nominated by the party authority is just a funny situation. Looking through the manifestoes of the various parties, it comes out clearly that except for promises to take up programmes for women's welfare, no political party has looked into the actual issue of empowerment of women in spite of pressure exerted by the national and international movements of women and the various pledges made by the Governments in the United Nations and other such fore. In State Legislative Assembly elections maximum candidates are contesting as independent candidates. During the Manipur State Legislative Assembly Election 1984, out of total five candidates four are independent and Smt. Joymati Devi of Sagolband constituency was the only party candidate (Congress). In Manipur, for the Inner Manipur Parliamentary election, out of the four proposed candidates of the BJP, one woman party member, O. Indira Devi is one of the hopeful candidates, but the party president recommended only one male candidate who is recently retired from the service. Reason may be different, but the most important one may be the gender factor. So, a group of women protested in front of the party office on 19th February, 2014 and they said that the matter will be informed to the party president at the centre.[7] But nothing happened in their movement. The party ticket was given to the male candidates.

The parties are usually against taking a risk of putting up women as candidates because of the social attitudes which disfavour women's entry into politics. Successful women candidates, numerically, are beyond the hope, because the entire game of power is generated through party organization, which is dominated by male leaders. The experience of India's sixty nine years periodic elections shows the inability of parties to make a place for the women. Due to the smaller percentage of women, presence of women does not result in any significant changes in either the nature of women's functioning or in the party approach to women and women's issues. Before the elections the parties put forth their principles in their manifestoes, indicating their policy perspectives. The manifestoes of all political parties contain promises of taking up programmes for the welfare of women. The issues of women become one of the important topics for capturing power through election. Candidates and parties not only used the issues of women as included in their manifestoes; they are also trying to use women as a weapon for winning the battle. In Manipur, candidates of different political parties wooed the voters with different activities which have been changing from election to election. During the election 2007 and 2012, women formed self-help groups (SHG) under the guidance of the active workers of party candidates. With the formation of such SHGs, women can get funds but the important motives behind the screen are to woo the voters for their party candidates. As a response to such activities of the party candidate, women in group show their respect to the candidates by bringing rice, vegetable, fruits etc. (so called Athenpot in Manipuri) during the public meeting. Local Meira Paibi units are the soft targets for every candidate. One critical condition in the present trend is women are coming to the voters with money on behalf of the candidates where male workers cannot enter. The maximization of the number of female voters has led various parties into paying greater attention to organizing the women and campaigning among them. In the past, such efforts were made only at the time of election, in the form of certain "popularistic and opportunistic short-term" promises. In accordance with the changed circumstances, the parties have established regular party forums, cells etc. for mobilizing women and seeking their supports, e.g. formation of Mahila Congress, Mahila Morcha etc. However, in the present political process of entry into decision-making political institutions, there is growing influence of money and muscle power, backroom dealings, communalization and criminalization. Due to this, many women have left political parties and formed informal women's groups.[8] Even during the election, the individual women's preferences are subdued by the choice of elders in the family, influential leaders etc. Here, one pity mindset of women has also been witnessing that they cannot show their choice against the choice of the elder male members of the family—husband, brother, father etc., just in the form of social obligation. As women remain at the periphery of the power structure, they lack the political consciousness needed to formulate and implement policies in accordance with the aspirations of women. Their presence as a candidate and as a voter is just a mere symbolism rather than real power wielding. Indian democracy, unfortunately, lacks the effective participation of all its citizens.

Participation of Women in the Electoral Politics of Manipur

Manipur merged to the Indian Union in 1949 as a Part C State. From the beginning of the Indian Parliamentary Election, Manipur women joined in the electoral politics. In the Parliamentary and Electoral College Election 1952, Manipuri women had participated as voters and candidates. Smt. Iswari Devi W/o late Maharaja Bodhachandra Singh contested in the Inner Manipur Parliamentary Constituency as an Independent candidate. But she got 11,809 votes only and was not elected. She was defeated by L. Jugeshwar Singh, who got 22,902 votes out of 75,586.[9] M.K. Binodini Devi contested from Khurai Constituency in the Electoral College election as an All Manipur National Union candidate and she got elected after defeating her three rivals. She secured 1970 votes out of 4,659 votes polled.

In the territorial council elections, another women Smt. Sabi Devi, who played a very active part in the women's movement of 1939, contested as a communist candidate from Wangkhei Kongba Constituency but was defeated. There were five candidates including her. She secured only 484 votes out of 9906 total votes polled.[10] Since, no women were elected in the Territorial Council election the then Chief Commissioner nominated two women members in the Territorial Council to ensure women's participation under the Union Territories Act, 1956. The nominated members were R.K. Mukhara Devi and Akim Annal in 1957; R.K. Mukhara Devi and Lhingjaneng Gangte in 1962; A. Bimola Devi and R.T. Shinny in 1967.[11] The next Territorial Council Election was held in 1962 along with the Parliamentary Election in the Inner and Outer Manipur Constituencies. As there was no elected women member, again,

Chief Commissioner of Manipur nominated R.K. Mukhara Devi and Lhingjaneng Gangte as members of the Territorial Council of Manipur.

Table 5.1: Party-wise Position of Elections in Manipur before Statehood

Sl. No.	Year	Congress	Socialist	Communist	Independent	Total
1.	1952	10	1	2	17	30
2.	1957	12	6	4	8	30
3.	1962	16	5	—	10	30
4.	1967	16	4	1	9	30

In July 1963, the Territorial Council of Manipur was converted into a Union Territory. The first Assembly Election of Manipur Union Territory was held in the early part of 1967 along with the Parliamentary Election. Smt. A. Bimola Devi and R.T. Shinny were nominated as members and the nominees joined the Congress Party. In these elections female voters outnumber the male voters in Manipur, i.e. in 1957 out of the total electorate of 330211, number of female voters were 168874. Again in 1967, out of the total 468707, only 231310 were male voters. This trend continued in this State. In the outer Parliamentary seat election 2014—the total number of female voters was 463068, while the number of male voters was 448631 only. In the inner Parliamentary seat again 437755 were female and only 415314 were male.

In almost all the elections, Parliamentary as well as State Legislative Assembly, women voters' outnumbered male voters in the State of Manipur. The following Table 5.2 shows the exact figure of male and female voters in Manipur from 1972 to 1984.

Table 5.2: Male and Female Voters in Manipur from 1972 to 1984

Year	Male	Female	Total
1972	2,87,563	3,08,279	5,95,842
1974	3,57,142	3,62,982	7,20,124
1980	4,37,620	4,71,650	9,09,262
1984	5,09,308	5,04,370	10,13,678

Source: Office file, Election Office, Lamphel Pat, Imphal.

According to the ratio of the male-female voters, the political parties cannot neglect value of the women voters in Manipur. But unluckily, during the filing of the nomination paper the attitude of the party authorities towards women is out of expectation and the same condition is happening during the declaration of the result for the few women candidates. The following Table 5.3 shows the female candidates along with the number of votes polled by them and the name of the political parties:

Table 5.3: Female candidates

Sl. No.	*Name of the women candidate*	*Party*	*Year*	*Constituency*	*Votes polled*
1.	R.K. Mukhara Devi	Congress	1972	Keisamthong	1655
2.	A. Bimola Devi	MPP	1972	Kontha	1301
3.	Lhingjaneng Gangte	Congress	1972	Henglep	3177
4.	A. Bimola Devi	MPP	1973	Heingang	2859
5.	Lhingjaneng Gangte	Congress	1973	Saikot	2590
6.	T. Kholly	Independent	1973	Saikot	2121
7.	W. Joymati Devi	Congress	1980	Sagolband	378
8.	R.K. Mukhara Devi	Congress	1980	Keisamthong	1381
9.	Kh. Bilashini Devi	CPI	1980	Bishnupur	1245
10.	M. Puinyabati Devi	Congress	1980	Thangmeiband	378
11.	A. Bimola Devi	Janata Dal	1980	Heingang	1947
12.	T. Kholly	Independent	1980	Saikot	2814
13.	Lhingjaneng	Janata Dal	1980	Saitu	2426
14.	Aribam Bimola Devi	Independent	1984	Heingang	1608
15.	W. Joymati Devi	Congress	1984	Sagolband	601
16.	N. Shyama Devi	Independent	1984	Lamlai	95
17.	Ngainu Vaiphei	Independent	1984	Jiribam	25
18.	Manlianniang	Independent	1984	Churachandpur	160

Source: Office file, Election Office, Lamphel Pat, Imphal.

Women voters outnumbered male voters in almost all the parliamentary and State legislative assembly elections, but up to 1990 no women MLA was elected in Manipur. They have been contesting the election through different political parties and as independent candidates. The first women elected in the

Manipur State Legislative Assembly was Smt. Hangmila, W/o Late Yangmaso Shaiza, Ex C.M. in 1990. Second was Smt. K. Apabi Devi W/o K. Bira Singh, who expired in the plane crash. She was the Minister of State in Manipur. Third was W. Leima Devi W/o W. Angou Singh, Ex M.P. in 2000. Fourth and present is O. Landhoni Devi W/o O. Ibobi Singh, C.M of Manipur in 2007 from Khangabok constituency. The participation of these women in the electoral politics of Manipur is also just a shadow of their husbands. Here, I want to mean is Hangmila Shaiza of Ukhrul Constituency captured the seat of her husband as a sympathy vote after the death of Sri Yangmaso Shaiza, the former Chief Minister of Manipur. Smt. Apabi Devi from Oinam constituency captured the seat of her husband when her husband Sri Bir Singh expired in plane crash as a sitting MLA. Smt. W. Leima Devi got the seat of her husband when he went to the Parliament. Smt. O. Landhoni Devi won the seat of her husband; Sri O. Ibobi Singh left the seat when he became the Chief Minister.

In the State Legislative Assembly Election 2007, in all the categories—Scheduled Tribe, Scheduled Caste and General women voters outnumbered the male voters, but number of contestants and elected women was only for namesake. The following Table 5.4 shows the exact figure of male and female as candidates, voters and elected too.

Table 5.4: Total number of Voters in Manipur State Legislative Assembly 2007

Categories	*Male*	*Female*	*Total*
General	489473	539531	1029004
S.C.	11541	12432	23973
S.T.	323355	330872	654227
Total	**824369**	**882835**	**1707204**

Source: Official Record of the Election Office, Lamphel Pat, Imphal.

Again, the total number of voters in 2012 Manipur State Legislative Assembly Election was 1741581, out of which 851540 are male and 890041 female. There was a difference of 34501 between male and female voters. Voter turn out in this

Table 5.5: Total number of Votes polled in 2007

Categories	*Male*	*Female*	*Total*	*Per cent*
General	4,21,907	4,76,391	8,98,208	87.29
S.C.	9,409	10,406	19,815	82.66
S.T.	2,76,673	2,79,814	5,56,487	85.06
Total	**7,07,989**	**7,66,521**	**14,74,510**	**86.37**

Source: Official Record of the Election Office, Lamphel Pat, Imphal.

Table 5.6: Total number of Contestants in the Manipur State Legislative Assembly Election 2007

Categories	*Male*		*Female*		*Total*	
	Contested	*Elected*	*Contested*	*Elected*	*Contested*	*Elected*
General	194	38	8	1	202	39
S.C.	5	1	0	0	5	1
S.T.	97	20	4	0	101	20
Total	**296**	**59**	**12**	**1**	**308**	**60**

Source: Official Record of the Election Office, Lamphel Pat, Imphal.

election was 1392596 (79.96%) out of which 694893 were female and 631223 male. There was a difference of 63670. The total number of contestants was 264, out of which 252 are male and 12 female. 57 male and 3 female were elected. INC captured 42 seats out of 60 within the critical situation created by a joint group of underground organizations, i.e. CORCOM, which created different problems including the lost of lives at the residence of the INC candidate (I. Hemochandra of Singjamei).

A new history opened with the election result of Manipur State Legislative Assembly Election 2012. A.K. Mirabai became the first women Cabinet Minister in the Manipur State Legislative Assembly. Nemcha Kipgen (MSCP) from Kangpokpi constituency and A.K. Mirabai (Congress I) from Patsoi constituency were elected, who came from the families which have no politician in their families before they were elected. In the parliamentary electoral history of Manipur only one woman M.P. was elected so far (Kim Gangte).

In the 2009 Lok Sabha election, the number of women who cast their votes in the North-East might have been more than the national average, but there were just 18 women candidates in the fray in the seven states against 538 in the rest of the 28 States and Union Territories. Nationally, 59 women finally entered the Lok Sabha and among them two were from Assam and one from Meghalaya. Among the seven States in the region, only Assam, Manipur, Meghalaya and Tripura had seen women candidates in the fray while Arunachal Pradesh, Mizoram, and Nagaland had drawn a blank in terms of woman candidate, two of them went to become Ministers, while Nationalist Congress Party MP from Tura Constituency—Agatha Sangma was Minister of State for Rural Development before she was sacked in 2012. Later on Congress MP from Lakhimpur in Assam, Ranu Narah was inducted into the Union Minister as Minister of States for Tribal Welfare. The third woman MP from region are Bijaya Chakravarty from Guwahati Constituency—she was Union Water Resources Minister in the previous NDA regime and presently BJP's National Vice President.

Local self-government is a good room for all citizens to take part in the decision-making process of the Government of the respective countries. During the British Colonialism for the first time decentralized (local self-government) was introduced in India in 1903. When the Britishers left India as an independent country, the value of democratic decentralization was seriously enshrined in the mind of the political leaders, Constitution makers, bureaucrats etc. Women have been taking part in the *panchayat* elections right from the beginning. Without any reservation women have contested in the *panchayats*. The importance of women's participation in the political process has been increasingly highlighted from different angles. So, the questions of reservation have come up. The first election with the reserved seats for women was held in 1978 after the Panchayati Raj Act, 1975. Women contested in both reserved and unreserved seats. After the introduction of the 73rd Amendment Act, 1992, Manipur Panchayati Raj Act, 1994 was passed with a remarkable episode of 33 per cent seats reserved for women. The government might have reserved 33 per cent of the *panchayat* seats for women are just for namesake. In many of the women reserved *panchayats*, husbands or any other male members of the family in this minority dominated locality who actually run the everyday affairs on behalf of their wives or any women relatives. So, it is quite clear that political platforms are dominated by man folk in the society with different changes.

Political Participation of Women

Women have an apathetic attitude towards electoral politics due to different socio-economic factors. Even though there is lesser figure in the electoral scenario, women participated in the political process through different angles. Political participation includes all the political acts through which people effected directly to the political decision-making process. It includes such activities as strikes, demonstration, sit in protests, mass movements, marches, presentation of memoranda as well as violent acts design to change the political system or the unconventional political activities. In Manipur such activities are performed by the women so actively. In the history of women's movement in Manipur, mention may be made that quite a few *maharanis* took active part in the administration during monarchical period. The king as well as the people sometimes sought the opinion or support of the women to solve difficult problems or situations which affected the interests of the community. In the history of Manipur there were many evidences where the king took the opinion and suggestions of their *maharanis* in matters of public interests. Sometimes, women in group gathered and complained to the king for correction, if he acted unruly and done any injustice.[12] As a matter of fact, the position of women is just in a puzzle situation. They are very active in social life, but they are not in decision-making. They organized different movements, giving pressure to the Government and Non-governmental organizations too. Their way of agitationist movement is quite typical in certain occasions. But they are not available or hardly available in the position of leadership in general.[13] Irom

Sharmila Chanu has been fasting against the Armed Forces Special Power Act for the last more than twelve years as a full right citizen of a parliamentary democratic country. There are millions of young girls who languish as they do not have the key to open the door of opportunities for progress. More and more women are getting involved in career building in the communication sector, but nominal or only few have been able to reach the position of decision-making level or to serve on governing bodies or boards. Women should be empowered through enhancing their skills, knowledge and access to modern science and information technology. Concerted efforts need to be taken up to tap the unrecognized and dormant human resources of the women section and to bring the women at the forefront of the decision-making process.

Conclusion

Although the policies and programmes of the Government seem to be quite useful and effective on papers, the Government must take necessary steps to implement these policies at the grassroots level. The implementing authorities or officials are to be made accountable for every action they take. Because, in spite of all the efforts made by the political decision-makers, the long established beliefs and notions about female inferiority and the social prescription and prohibitions build around them have proved a hard nut to crack and as a result, women find it difficult to use the existing facilities to remove the hindrances of equality. A Bill on women reservation of seats is also lying in the Parliament. The political equality guaranteed by the democratic constitutions in the form of fundamental rights, political rights etc. is not able to penetrate deeply in the social roots in spite of many policies and programmes of the Government. The women should not be let to believe that political activity is inappropriate for her. This change in the psyche of women would definitely affect the women's interest in politics and public affairs resulting in a change in the level of political participation of women. In the social life the bias against women and girl child has to be fought by social movements and by ensuring freedom to women from the oppressive social codes. Both men and women will have to work together in this direction, so that, human resources are not wasted or exploited by the brutal forces.

Notes

1. Kapur, A.C., 1981, *Principles of Political Science*, S. Chand & Company Ltd., New Delhi, pp. 428-29.
2. Chattopadhyay, Tapan Kumar, 2008, Voluntary Action and Women Emancipation, in Ray, B. Dutta and Ray, Asok Kumar (eds.) *Women Emancipation, Focus North-East India*, Om Publication, New Delhi, p. 325.
3. *Times of India* (National Daily), Dt. 17.02.2014, p. 6.
4. Johari, J.C., 1983, *Indian Government and Politics*, Vishal Publication, Delhi, p. 824.
5. Kosambi, Meera, 2000, Women, Emancipation and Equality, in Thorner Alice and Krishnaraj Maithreyi (Eds.), *Ideals, Images and Real Lives*, Sameeksha Trust, Hyderabad, p. 139.
6. Khanna, Manuka, 2009, Political Participation of Women in India, *The Indian Journal of Political Science*, Volume LXX, No. 1, January-March, p. 60.
7. *Poknapham* (Imphal, Manipuri Local), Dt. 20.02.2014, p. 1.
8. Thokchom, Binarani Devi, 2011, *Women's Movement in Manipur*, Concept Publishing Company Pvt. Ltd., New Delhi, p. 196.
9. Election Results 1952, Office of the Chief Electoral Officer, Imphal.
10. Singh, R.P., 1981, *Electoral Politics in Manipur*, Concept Publishing Company, New Delhi, p. 21.
11. Singh, P. Bharat, 1997, *Elections in Manipur*, P. Mirabai Devi, Imphal, pp. 10-13.
12. Singh, L. Ibungohal, 1960, *An Introduction to Manipur*, Imphal, p. 31.
13. Th. Binarani Devi, 2012, Politics and Women Empowerment; North-East India Context, *India Journal of Development Research*, Vol. 4, No. 3, July-December, p. 55.

6

Women in Democracy and Peace Processes

The democratic government has a great responsibility to create favourable socio-economic and political atmosphere for the empowerment of women, making them capable citizen of the state to discharge their duties in a positive and rightful manner. Democracy is a fundamental aspect of human development. The test of government is the welfare of the people, and that form of government is to be preferred which gives to human tendencies the fullest scope for development. The primary functions of a democratic government are similar to those of any other form of government. But in addition to this, democracy stimulates to self-education, for participation in governmental activities, open wider horizons for the individual and leads to broadened interests. The lessons of democracy are liberty, fraternity and rationality. Its principle is that all persons who are fit to perform the duties of citizens should have a share in the direction of the State, so that, each man may have an identical opportunities to grow and expand to the best of her capacity, and there is no man or group of men who will exploit the weakness of others. Democracy does not differentiate between man and man, man and woman, rich and poor, and high and low. It raises the common man high on the pedestal of social and political glory and this is the meaning of the government of the people. It promised the enjoyment of equal political rights for all as candidates as well as voters in the electoral process and equal participation in the decision-making process of the State. Democracy ensures that everyone has the opportunity to exercise their rights and to participate politically, economically, socially and culturally in their respective societies. Then it will create the society which has equal participation of all people, and active use of their rights (with respect for the rights of others) helps to strengthen democracy by ensuring the accountability and legitimacy of the State. It requires sustaining people's rights to equality and non-discrimination, to express their views, to choose their governments, to a fair trial, and to the full enjoyment of all other human rights. Democratic societies require constant political commitment from those in power to promote and respect human rights and deepening democracy. This requires participating in political processes to commit themselves to be bound by the rules that regulate democratic societies—'the rule of the game'. Government must be prepared to accept the will of the people, even if it means political defeat, and to accommodate divergent views and needs in society.[1] It also encourages the establishment of institutions, legal guarantees and protections for the full exercise of human rights. This in turn creates a stable and secure environment and greater opportunities for individuals to flourish. Due to gendered socialization, women are not allowed to participate in the decision-making process and remained as silent victims to the discrimination, violation of their rights, issues of domestic violence, harassment which the societal customs and culture made natural happenings for women. In order to fight against the various discriminations, the participation of women in political process is very important. Due to the existing gender inequalities, women require active Governmental support for their social, political and economic upliftment and empowerment. But in all democratic countries of the world, women participating in the decision-making process are found to be less than men. Measuring progress is inherently difficult because progress towards democracy has been found in a mixed situation. Women, which have been relegated to secondary status is not only absolutely false, but is the result of illicit generalization. Their contribution is both in theory and practice. Women are struggling, demanding and fight for the just cause with any issue or problem from time-to-time and place-to-place. They are no more remaining as passive spectators. They are coming out and take a lead.

But within the framework of democratic societies in this ongoing global scenario and sixty-four years after the declaration of Universal Declaration on Human Rights people are suffering the problems of the violation of human rights. The issue of governance may be considered as more important than others for the creation of rightful and conducive atmosphere, not only for women themselves, but also for the society at large. Both men and women have become victims of violence. Many innocent people have lost their lives due to the violence created by both state and non-state actors. In the name of the maintenance of law and order and for bringing welfare to the society, a number of draconian laws have been enforced causing untold suffering of the masses. In a democratization process, there should be an obligation for policy-makers and security forces to be accountable to the public for their decision and actions.

Women have long been active in lobbying and organizing for peace and disarmament. Grassroots women's groups have organized across party and ethnic lines, advocating for peace and carrying out reconciliation efforts. They have called for the elimination of weapons of mass destruction, campaigned against small arms, participated in weapons collection programmes and disseminated information on landmines. Mothers have organized to learn the fate of their 'disappeared children' or to prevent their children from being conscripted or sent to war. The activities of the civil society women organizations are not an end in itself. It is a means to an end. They can perform only the input function in the political process. If their activities are not responded by the government, they shattered off. Women organization has had to continually face new issues and challenges in these ongoing years. Issues have arisen that have challenged the understanding and certitude of the past, forcing all of us to rethink our position and convictions to our duties. The women's movement challenges the police and judiciary primarily as patriarchal structure of power exhibited in the activities of the government, and reshapes the potential of a powerful community of women who would in turn be tied against an unjust social order. This applies the North-East too and the women's movement in the region needs to become a part of similar movement at the national level.

Peace building efforts are anti-hegemonic projects in that they seek not so much to replace existing power structures with different ones, but to supplant the need for any hegemonic power structure to take roots in the first place. It decentralizes notions of power and agency, and thus brings together those who were previously marginalized by hegemonic structures and empowers them through more egalitarian relations. Peacekeeping operation is no longer limited to military activities (both state and non-state). These activities may have broad mandates to assist in elections, monitor human rights and carry out police functions. They may help to develop legal institutions, create administrative structures, establish mine action programme, repatriate refugees and deliver humanitarian aid. Multidimensional peacekeeping operations have a great potential for addressing issues of the violation of human rights due to the ethnic and armed conflicts. Such operations have a profound impact on people's lives. In India, women activism is registered in the historical struggle for nationalism, worker's right and struggles based on social issues. In the North-East the women have a rich history of their involvement in the insurgency affected areas. The collective empowerment and organized movements for common cause is the need of the day. The collective movement of such nature requires not only organization at the local level, but also need network organizations at the national and international levels. Women's movement could countervail the state power. There is a real need to show organizational strength for making the state take proactive role in favour of women. Insensitive way in which the state addresses movements was also seen when a case of attempted suicide was lodged against Medha Patkar when she sat on fast to protect against the raising of the level of the Narmada Dam.[2]

Women's Contribution in the Process of Peace and Harmony (in Group)

Women delved into public action to promote internal and domestic peace and to contain violence in the family and community. The imbalance surface within the existing inter-relationship between the ethnic groups, between the indigenous and the outsiders; between the state and the non-state actors etc. threw a big challenge not only to the institutions, but also to the basic structure of the Indian states. On the other hand the state still views the problems of insurgency in the North-East as a governance problem. Guided by such view the state has taken recourse to force and counter-insurgency measures through military and para-military concentration. Keeping in view the duty of the Union under Art. 355 of the Constitution, *inter alia* to protect every state against internal disturbance, it is considered desirable that the Central Government should also have power to declare areas as 'disturbed', to enable its armed forces to exercise the special powers. Areas declared 'disturbed' under the Armed Forces Special Power Act (AFSPA) over the past 50 years vary significantly according to their conflict history, ethnic constituency, and levels of militancy. These have sensationalized the civic community and affected their civil rights in a big way. All the areas where this act is imposed share a common experience of widespread human rights abuses. The AFSPA has also had the opposite effect in each state where the AFSPA has been implemented and soldiers have been deployed; the armed forces have become a symbol of oppression and an object of hate. So, the movement against this Act is one of the burning issues at present.

There are some notable women organizations like Matri Manch, Sajagota Samiti, Bodo Women Justice Forum etc. which exhibit their activities when there is any issue in the society. During the last two decades thousands of people lost their lives with different forms of violent incidents in Assam. With the beginning of 1970s, the Government of India in order to suppress the underground outfit deployed armed forces in Assam and carried out massive military operations such as Operation Rhino, Operation Bajarang, Operation Golden Bird etc. which resulted massive human rights violation. When any incident of violence or the violation of human rights, mainly violence against women takes place, such as rape, police raids, The Sajagota Mahila Samiti (a loose knit women organization of Assam) immediately get organized and lead protest march and agitated for the restoration of human rights. In connection with the activities of the Samiti, they are quite independent, they received no support from any angle, e.g. state or non-state actors. But this organization is so active when there is an issue or problem in the State.

The tradition of Meitei women's powerful civil society organizations rising against oppressive measures of the State and also against social evils is quite evident even today. In fact, Meira Paibi in course of time became a public platform and different women organizations in different localities of Manipur use this platform for protection of human rights of the innocent civilians and for protection of the women communities from atrocities committed by the State. In recent times they have been agitating against the Armed Forces Special Power Act operating in Manipur. This movement is mainly because of the Government used different Acts in connection with the maintenance of law and order in the State. AFSPA is also one among them which is giving a serious blow to the normal life of the people. Instead of the maintenance of law and order, with the mask of this Act, the State forces and the Indian Army killed and arrested a number of people, including innocent ones. The association is fighting with the atrocities of the Armed Personnel with different Acts and Bills in the State of Manipur. The world famous naked protest in front of the Assam Rifles Forces against the custodial rape and killing of Ms. Manorama of Imphal East by the Assam Rifles on 11th July, 2004 was a remarkable protest performed by the women of All Manipur Social Reformation and Development (a women voluntary organization of Manipur, established in 1974-75 and it became a registered body in 1977-78 (Reg. No. 2441). On 10th December, 2008, under the leadership of Smt. K. Taruni Devi, President of the association formed a group called 'Sharmila Kanba Lup' at PDA Complex Porompat. Their motto is to support Sharmila and demand to remove AFSPA from Manipur. A continuous relay hunger strike is still going on from different parts of the State.[3]

Women from various ethnic communities have emerged as major social actors to fight against the grave social injustice and have developed their own capabilities to effectively address such situations. Although the women of North-Eastern Region have been playing very significant roles in peace-making, their roles are either being ignored or their capacities for peace-building are not recognized and utilized. In most cases it is seen that the Governments are not coming freely for any open discussion and normalization process. If happened so, it takes a long process and time. The State-led peace initiatives could not make any breakthrough in spite of different accords signed between the Government and the rebel organizations. In such circumstances the civil society organizations in the State came forward with peace initiatives, but they are not invited/included as a part of the peace talks between the Government and the rebel organizations. It seems to me that women are often excluded from formal peace processes because they are not decision-makers, military leaders or combatants, or because it is assumed they lack the necessary skills (underestimation). But these women civil society organizations appealed for peace dialogues between the Government and the underground organizations. Peace processes fail to take gender perspectives into account. The roles of the women organizations in the North-East India in general and Manipur in particular are historically and politically significant. The movement and activism of the women in the region for the protection of human rights show the serious concern of the civil society organizations in peace building and human rights protection. They come out in a very impartial manner and they may foster peace-making efforts and become active peacemaker. This attitude and action of women in North-East India has been embodied in the history and culture of the region, e.g. with the passage of time the way of practices may be changed, but the women in Tangkhul society still preserving their culture and traditions. The NSCN (IM) and the Assam Rifles developed a situation of tension at Siroy Village of Ukhrul District. The NSCN (IM) signed the cease fire agreement with Government of India in Nagaland. But they have their designated camps at Ukhrul, Senapati and Chandel Districts of Manipur. The stand-off between Assam Rifles and the NSCN (IM) began on Sunday (18th January) night when soldiers of the country's oldest para-military force surrounded the banned outfit's camp at Kuisumong. They asked the rebels to vacate the area saying the cease-fire was only limited to Nagaland and no such camps were allowed in Manipur. The Naga Militants, however, refused to abide by the Assam Rifles' order and threatened to retaliate if the 'camp' was attacked.[4] In such armed conflict situation of Siroy area, Tangkhul women came out and demanded scaling down of security forces and guerrillas. They make a vigil all the time during the tension and requested to both the parties and gave the massage of their motherly feelings and importance of the feeling of brotherhood to all the people. Lastly, the NSCN (IM) left the area and normalcy brought.

The Naga Mothers' Association a voluntary social organization of Nagaland was founded on February 14, 1984 out of the Naga Women's deep concern for the increasing socio-political problems in Naga Society. This organization is a non-political body which is trying to take an independent stand and to negotiate with the State, armies and the rebels for the cause of peace. In the year 1994 the Naga Mothers' Association found the peace team with the slogan "Shed no more blood" and initiated dialogue with the State government and rebel groups to stop violence and bloodshed.[5] The most important thing about the Naga Mothers' Association is that it tried to deal with the root causes of conflicts in order to bring about positive peace. Naga Mothers' Association identified underdevelopment of the people as the root cause of any conflict and tried to address the issue by undertaking programmes for development such as health, drug abuse, alcoholism etc. that paralyzed the development of the people and threw them to deeper frustration. The Naga women have channelized their customary role by appealing for peace as mothers, wives and sisters.

Ethnic and inter-ethnic conflicts are the common happenings of socio-political and economic history of North-East India as a gift of the excluded and partly excluded policy of the British Colonial administration; and as well as the increasing strategic location at the interface of diametrically opposite ideological regimes, value systems, heterogeneous cultural landscapes, and currents of civilizations. Moreover, multiplicity of cultures, material existence, economic lives along with the phenomenal intra-spatial variations in the form of dense forest, high hills and narrow valleys, mighty barriers created by the rivers, torrential rains, recurrent tremors in the absence of adequate means of intra- and inter-regional linkage etc. have contributed in keeping people too much confined to their narrow territorial and parochial imperatives with little scope for inner dynamism and change. Due to the lack of acknowledgement and actions of the existing Government from time-to-time, the frustration and alienation among the people of different communities increased day-by-day. Tolerance, understanding, and negotiations are the important weapons for resolving such conflicts by the voluntary organizations of different communities at the organizational level. So, Naga Mothers' Association tried to have a good network with other organizations of other communities for stopping the ethnic conflict for upholding the finest social ethics of the North-Eastern Indian States' culture. They organized number of awareness programmes in various villages on anti-drug trafficking.

In Manipur different women associations took up the task of *Nasha Bandi* means to stop drugs and alcohols. But those drunkards who were handed over to the local police were released without taking any action as the discretion of higher ups. In this regard the All Manipur Social Reformation and

Development Samaj requested to the then Governors and Ministers of the State by submitting memos. But these were only submission of 'memos' and request. The existing Government remained in a deaf ear. So, the association decided to start a movement with different forms of pressures to the existing Governments. Government may collect taxes but what are the social problems which are happening after having alcohol, need to take into account. As a result of the demand and pressure of the association, the Manipur State Legislative Assembly has introduced the Bill of 'Prohibition' in 1991. At present AIDS/HIV infected persons are increasing at an alarming rate in Manipur. For giving awareness and sensitization to the rural areas they organized seminars, conferences, meetings etc.[6] They are of the opinion that maximum crimes in Manipur are happening as a result of the using alcohol and drugs by the men folk. After using alcohol and drugs, they committed a lot of violent actions to the family members, especially to their wives and children. If they have no money for buying alcohol and drugs they asked to their wives and children or to their parents by the unmarried youth. If they are not getting up to these conditions they tried to steel household properties like jewellery. With the influence of alcohol and drugs they commit crimes and fighting among themselves.

Case Study-I

Sri Khundrakpam Shyamkisor Sing of Khurai Ahongei, Imphal East District of Manipur killed his wife Khundrakpam (Ongbi) Sanahanbi Devi on 8-4-93. All the women sections of Manipur soaked the incidents and protested from all directions. In this case also, the All Manipur Social Reformation and Development Samaj took a leading role and the culprit was arrested and put into jail. A campaign for safeguarding and killing of innocent women was launched and demanded the action against the real culprit by the women of Manipur under the leadership of All Manipur Social Reformation and Development Samaj. They submitted a memorandum to the Chief Minister of Manipur on 11 April, 1993.

Case Study-II

An innocent five years small boy of Singjamei Thongam Leikai of Imphal West District, Manipur, was killed on 24th April, 1987 by his two neighbour drug addicts for just a small earring worth Rs. 180 only. For this merciless killing, the All Manipur Social Reformation and Development Samaj organized meetings, processions, to draw public sentiments and also pursuing the Government to punish the wrong doers.

There are a number of gender crimes, rape cases, molestation, killing etc. in Manipur too. On 24-1-1986, Miss Luingamla Muinao of Ukhrul District was mercilessly murdered by two army personels and again on 8-3-1986, Km. Neelam Panchabhaiya discovered dead half floating in the Imphal River in a suspicious manner. People raised hue and cry throughout the State in these cases. The All Manipur Social Reformation and Development Samaj took a leading role along with other frontal organizations like AMSU, MSF etc. They submitted a memorandum to the Hon'ble Prime Minister on 18-3-86. They have requested to look into the matter and requested to punish the alleged two army personnels mentioned in the memo and demanded a judicial enquiry into the case of Neelam Panchabhaiya, to bring out the real culprits. Raped and mercilessly killing of Km. Kunjarani Devi and Km. R.K. Tamphasana Devi make a great soak to the motherly feelings of the association. On 24-2-1992, one tribal widow, named Lalmalsomi, 35 years, ot Kom community, who have four children was captured by some Anti-Social Gang Groups. Her case was taken up by the association with the help of State Police forces and saved the life of innocent widow in time. The Gang Party was also arrested by the State Police force.[7]

As a result of social evils like drug addict, alcoholism, human trafficking etc. a number of crimes are witnessing in the region. Such brutal action does not left even women and children. In connection with the killing of an innocent girl at Kohima, Lochumbino, Secretary General of Naga Mothers' Association, said that such senseless and ruthless act of targeting on an innocent girl has no place in Naga Society and could not be accepted by the Naga mothers. Questioning the 'right and authority' of the gunman in shooting at a girl, Naga Mothers' Association urged all the value of human lives. The Association appealed the law enforcing agencies to keep vigil in and around the capital, so that, such incidents should not be occurred again besides demanding the arrest of the culprits. Naga Mother's Association acknowledges the importance of individual and group efforts (non-governmental) in this regards. They received S. Bidyalaxmi Leima, a Manipuri women Cyclist, who was in a tour in North-East India with a slogan to create awareness on violence against women, during the first weak of September 2013. During the occasion, with the increasing rate of rape, murder and violence against women in North-East India, the Association said, "we need to address the present social menace and introspect with all seriousness where society has gone wrong. There is also a need to change our mindset. We need to find out the root cause and family background of perpetrators and their families to access more knowledge and try to find remedial measures to curb the rising rate of all crimes" (*ToI*. 3-9-2013, p. 2).

In Assam, Matri Manch took up the issues of abuse of women both by the state and non-state actors during the insurgency problems. Women are the target of any group during the conflict situations that may be ethnic conflict or armed conflict. With the increasing scale of the issues of insurgency, mother lost their sons, sisters lost their brothers. Even girls also joined to the outfits. The concerns for their sons and daughters those who have disappeared or killed during the encounter with State police or Paramilitary forces led to the formation of Matri Manch in Assam. Of late those women, who are not mothers, also joined to the association with their motherly feelings. Men need to be taught to respect women right from their childhood. Violence against women needs to address rights from the grassroots level.

As an acknowledgement of the contributions made by the voluntary women organizations of North-East India, the Naga Mothers' Association of Nagaland and Meira Paibi of Manipur were awarded the *Times of India Social Award* in January 2013, which was handed over by the President of India.

As a matter of fact the activities of women for restoration of peace in Manipur are so important for understanding the socio-political and economic study of the State. Women, not in the form of above formal organizations, also come forward individually and voluntarily, they join together and launch movement for restoration of peace in the State from time-to-time. In politics and other social affairs, women of any community have been able to influence men in many ways directly or indirectly through the village councillor or at least through their husband. In the bygone days when head hunting was practiced, woman played a vital role in saving the lives of men. A woman of the village, during inter-village feuds and wars, would act as an ambassador, and a mediator. In such a case both the warring villages would recognize diplomatic women. The neutral lady—Phukhareila among the Tangkhul, could boldly enter a battle field and intervened between warring groups. She had the right of her own to intervene in the political and social affairs of the society; it is interfered with the general public.[8]

Individual Woman's Contribution in the Process of Peace and Harmony

More armed groups result in more small arms influx in the Indo-Burma border areas. Because of the existence of the outfits, small arms continue to proliferate in many parts of North-East Indian States. Many young persons have taken the path of violence resulting in death, decay and destruction in the social, political and economic fields. Many parts of South Asia, and especially North-East Indian States can be termed as fragmented societies that run on guns and drugs. There is a frightening influx of small arms and narcotic drugs in the region. The State and Central Governments treat the conflicts only as a law and order issue. Intrinsic to this approach is the Armed Forces Special Power Act, enacted by the Union Parliament as a temporary measure on 22nd May, 1958. It continues to be in force today. When it was enacted, the Naga National Council was the only major military group in North-East India. But today, even according to the Home Ministry there are more than 30 militant groups in this region. AFSPA has been ineffective in dealing with the problems, but there is resistance to its repeal though there are many allegations of violation of human rights with impunity.

Not only in group, individual movement of Irom Sharmila Chanu is also a notable one. People from different parts of the globe gave their support, but the Government paid no heed. Manipur created a new history of women's movement when Irom Sharmila launched hunger strike since November 4, 2000 in protest against killing of ten civilians at Malom by the Assam Rifles personnel following a bomb attack by the underground outfits on the armed personnel on 2nd November, 2000. Sharmila Chanu has been detained for continuing one year since 2001 with a charge of attempting to commit suicide under section 309 of the IPC. She has a confidence for the success of her movement, but it is only the time factor—quick or slow. She had mentioned this in front of the Media. AFSPA is a weapon of the weak, if the Government of India has a will, they should use their brain. Sharmila is force-fed through her nose. Her firm resolve to fast till the AFSPA is repealed has brought the issue of human rights violation into the public domain sparkling off a cloudburst of protest and reaction by human rights organizations. Being in a high security ward and hardly accessible even to her family members it is feared that Sharmila will be deliberately kept away from the world outside till she is too weak to even think of rights violation, leave alone fight against it. But no one and no effort can control Sharmila's zeal to fight against this draconian law and prevalence of the basic rights of the people. Even she shifted her hunger strike base to New Delhi for six months (October 2006 to March 2007).

G. Ananthapadmanabhan lead Amnesty International India visited Imphal recently as a part of their campaign across the country to seek Sharmila's unconditional release. The leader said Sharmila should not be punished for exercising her Constitutional rights and should be released immediately. As a matter of fact she has no intention to commit suicide. Her movement is only to protect innocent public from the draconian laws which is giving full power to the State forces. Imphal East Session Court released Sharmila Chanu on 20th August, 2014. Noted human rights lawyer Khaidem Mani appeared on behalf of Sharmila Chanu. A. Guneshwar Sharma, Judge of the Court said no evidence points to Sharmila trying to fast to death. She has been demanding repeal of the controversial Armed Forces Special Power Act 1958.[9]

The national leaders did not pay heed to her demand for removal of AFSPA 1958. The present NDA Government is also not ready to repeal the Armed Forces Special Power Act, 1958 even though the State and National BJP leaders were so vocal before the 2014 parliamentary election against the UPA Government by showing their sympathy on humanitarian ground for Sharmila Chanu related with her movement against this Act.

In Assam, violence dominated the social scenario with the beginning of 1970s with different underground and over ground movements. People experience the problems from both State and non-State actors. Dr. Mamoni Goswami requested the Central Government to control troops engaged in counter-insurgency operation against the outlawed ULFA in view of the current peace initiatives and to create a congenial atmosphere to bring the rebels to the negotiation table. With a motherly feeling, Dr. Mamoni Goswami spoke in the peace process and also stressed the need for extensive study of the problems that would help formulation of a holistic plan for amicable settlement of insurgency. With a relentless effort and conscious, the ULFA also agreed to send a nine member peoples' consultative group to initiate the discussion with the Central Government. Even though the issue is not, still, at a final stage, her effort could be regarded as the most important step towards attaining peace in the State.

In Myanmar (Burma), Aung San Suu Kyi, Burma's pro-democracy leader and Nobel Peace Laureate, has come to symbolize the struggle of Burma's people to be free and democratic rights for all. It was a time when there was mass slaughter of protestors by the brutal and unresponsive rule of the military strongmen Neh Win. She was determined to fight against the military regime in a non-violent way and started a non-violent struggle for democracy and human rights in Myanmar. The demand was for a change in the political system. The people wanted no more of the authoritarian rule initiated by a military camp in 1962. The discontent of the people for years had come to a boil in 1988. The military government tried to control the activities of NLD under the leadership of Aung San Suu Kyi. She has spent more than 15 years in detention, most of it under house arrest. Facing the increasing domestic and international pressures, the dictatorship was forced to call a general election, held in 1990. Aung San Suu Kyi was banned from personally standing in the election. As Aung San Suu Kyi began to campaign for the NLD, she and many others were detained by the regime. Despite conditions around the elections being far from free and fair with Aung San Suu Kyi and other democracy activists being detained, biased media, and intimidation of politicians, the voting on the day was relatively free and fair. The NLD won a staggering 82 per cent of the seats in Parliament. The dictatorship never recognized the results of the election, and refused to hand over power. National League for Democracy Party in Burma was banned on May 10, 2010. She was released from her current third period of detention on Saturday 13th November, 2010. Suu Kyi's ambition for restoration of democracy in Burma was supported internally as well as externally. Renowned international figures, who are interested in the protection and development of democracy met Suu Kyi and tried to know the existing conditions of democratic processes in Burma and around. She also received all the supports and cooperation with respect and understanding. Aung San Suu Kyi has won numerous international awards, including the Nobel Peace Prize, the Sakharov Prize from the European Parliament and the United States Presidential Medal of Freedom. She has called on people around the world to join the struggle for freedom in Burma, saying "Please use your liberty to promote ours." She was awarded, in absentia, the 1990 Rafto Human Rights Prize on

October 12, 1990 and the 1990 Sakharov Prize (human rights prize of the European Parliament). Suu Kyi was awarded the 1991 Nobel Peace Prize on October 14, 1991.

Women's movements have a great contribution in the socio-economic and political development of the society. They have dealt with the whole socio-political and economic conditions of the society. With the progress of civilization as well as experiences they also acknowledged about the position and the role of women. They also became aware of the fact that if the conditions of the women are not improved and aware, the welfare and development of the society will have no meaning. As they are contributing nearly halve of the total population, their role is very important in a democratic society. The women of Manipur are now politically conscious and often resort to various forms of agitations in a democratic way and trying to get the real meaning and fruits of democracy. In every demonstration, female participation constitutes about 50 per cent and above of the total populations. There are some movements that are launched by women only. In the mass movements too they think that their participation is compulsory. We can also observe at present that though women came out actively on many issues, they hardly succeed and attain their goal on some of the important social issues. One important factor responsible for their failure is the appeasing policy of the ruling party. Many political leaders often employed and misguided them for their interests and advantages. This created many factions and led to groupism. The other factor is the prevailing law and order situations in Manipur which hampers the execution of their work. The societal aspects of human aggregation are based on moral voluntaristic cooperative social processes. Coercive power, violence and conflicts do not explain a major part of societal existence. Therefore, it is argued that it is the non-violent, non-coercive power and normative voluntaristic behaviours that explain the existence and continuation of human society. The pressure and movements of Manipuri women in all the conflict situations tends, therefore, to be treated with certain derision or simply set aside as irrelevant. To counteract, many women movements became more aggressive, rude and more violent like radical who feel they must blow up everything to set things right. But, it should not create any negative impression upon the mind of the general public.

The fundamental prerequisite for reconstruction of human society on the foundations of peace is reduction in ego centrism, group centrism, and simultaneous altruism. There shall be no peace in the true sense of the world or survival of human kind in a dignified manner without developing greater and greater elements of altruism in human society. The only way to solve the problems of violence is to inculcate values of non-violence and develop altruistic personalities. With substantial increase in attitudes of love, compassion, kindness and sympathetic joy expressed through interactions and inter-relationships with individuals there is bound to be a qualitative improvement in social reality. A truly non-violent person radiates peace and peace values to others. Her very presence in a social group will be source of positive inspiration for others.

Targeted legislation and other interventions (education and employment) are necessary to overcome the legal and social barriers based on gender equality. Reduction and dismantling the State financial social services increase pressure on the private sector to undertake the functions, resulting in higher prices or unavailability of services and greater demands on women to make-up for lost services. The disruption of social networks caused by conflict contributed to growing numbers of marginalized groups, including war widows, orphans, the disabled, children and women heading households. The reconstruction of damaged or destroyed social sectors, including health, education and social services, are necessary to support long term social healing and integration. Counselling should be cultured and gender sensitive, involving local expertise and grounded in local realities.

Women's movements led to the democratization of society. In a democratization process, there should be an obligation for policy-makers and security forces to be accountable to the public for their decisions and actions. Demobilizing the combatants and reintegrating them into normal life is one of the most challenging priorities in post-conflict situations. In most cases, women are almost completely excluded from post-conflict decision-making processes. Women bring to peace process a practical understanding of real life and gender sensitivity. Today, peace process addresses the need for strengthening every democratic institutions and protecting human rights.

The larger women's organizations and parties are naturally subservient to the interests of the parent party or women's organization, and though there is a lot of talk of independent women organizations this does not in practice work out. It seems that women as a group have yet to develop the organizational and managerial skills to sustain any large organization or movement on their own and totally independent of men. In the North-East women are forced to be subordinate both from external pressure of the men-folk to conform to the community norms as well as due to lack of self-confidence. This may sound paradoxical in the North-East, in States like Meghalaya and Manipur whose women are economically and educationally advanced. Consultations with women's group and networks can provide insights on conflict situations. Understanding gender norms and customs in a society may prove important information for early warning. Women in peacekeeping missions may act as role models for local women in societies where women have traditionally played secondary roles. More women within military and police staff would facilitate contact with women and foster trust among the local population during the normal situation not only to take part in controlling the movements or agitations of the women groups.

Peacekeeping missions can benefit from contact with civil society, including women's organizations and network, to understand the specific impact of armed and ethnic conflict and the effect of peacekeeping operations on women and girls. Women peace movement often focus on shared experiences and produced solidarity across lines of division, which make it hard to cast the enemy as 'the other'. The concerns of these groups have about their children and other family members give them a social legitimacy and a linkage with women from different sides of the conflict. As a result, women have sometimes less difficulties than men in expressing concerns about a conflict. The area of work covered by the activities of women's group and network is not confining to a limited area of State or Country. Women's group and network have begun to work at regional or sub-regional area.

The counter-insurgency is indiscriminate, and affects the civic zones badly. On the other hand the militant terrorists in order to disseminate terrorism implicate the entire civil society and tend to universalized terrorism through their acts in public places. This causes casualities not only of the armed forces but also of the civilians. Thus, the powers, State and the insurgents had pressed the civil society and reduced the civic rights. The social and psychological cost of insurgency and counter-insurgency cannot be measured through in quantitative terms, increasing anxiety, unpredictability of life, liberty and fragile peace features in the State.

In today's insurgency and counter-insurgency affected Manipur 'Meira Paibi' (women torch bearer—night vigil group of women in Manipur) hold mashals and keep a watch in the neighbourhood where local youths are sometimes forcibly taken by armed personnels—both State and non-State forces, arrested and killed and giving charges of different crimes after killing. Sometimes, it is confused who had been killed by State forces or non-State forces, they are charging each others.

Conclusion

Women are taking a great role in the process of peace and stabilized society even though they are the target of the armed conflict situation. Their role in the development of a society is not only with women concerned, but for the sake of the whole society. These women are in the peace process because of their own initiatives only. When the State Government wants to involve them, the women are asked to play the role of healer but there has been no example of women being involved in the actual negotiation or post-conflict reconstruction. Women are perceived either as victims or as healers. Women in such situation are expected to uphold cultural and ethnic identities. Thus, in a situation of armed conflict there is marginalization of women's right as both the armed forces and military groups reinforced patriarchal values. In spite of demands from different angles women are not involved in the decision that affects them. To solve the problem of conflict care should be taken to foster a culture of peace that upholds justice and tolerance for all. To do this knowledge for promotion of peaceful conflict resolution have to be encouraged with sensitization, education, training, community action and youth exchange programme particularly for young women.

In actual fact, the effective and meaningful involvement of women in all the decision-making bodies—political, social and religion—is very crucial. If their strength, creativity and energy are to be harnessed along with their knowledge and skill, they have to be mainstreamed and empowered to choose their pathways of development. Obviously, they can exercise their choices best from a vantage position of power, prestige and knowledge. Therefore, they must be freed from the traditional barriers that hold women back from realizing their dreams and their full potentials. It is only them that we can talk about harnessing women power.

Traditional progressive values such as equality, dignity and freedom are central to women's struggle, but to limit the conceptualization of our politics to these existing parameters is to deny its deeper revolutionary implication. Feminist politics must extend earlier progressive values in ways that reflect the transforming presence of women on the political stage. We are not simply entering politics as it has existed. When fully half of the human race has been excluded from the practice and definition of politics, our entry necessarily transformed its very shape and definition. Women's entry into politics as women are in fact, the emergence of the long subordinate, devalued and marginalized sphere of private life and reproduction into the public and is an event of world historical significance. Any significant increase in women's participation and power in politics and production will require a concomitant change in the organization of the domestic sphere.

Notes

1. Tyagi, Suresh Kumar, 2012, *Human Rights and Democratization*, Swastic Publications, New Delhi, p. 7.
2. Biswas, Saswati, 2008, The Gender Concerns in North-East India and Relevance of Social Movements, in Ray, Basudev and Ray, Asok Kumar (eds.), *Women Emancipation, Focus North-East India,* Om Publication, New Delhi, p. 99.
3. *Interviewed* with Smt. K. Taruni Devi, President, All Manipur Social Reformation and Development Samaj.
4. *Times of India,* dt. 23-1-2009.
5. Phukan Dolly, 2007, Women in the Peace Process in North-East India, in Ray, Asok Kumar and Dev, B.J., (eds.) *Terrorism and Human Rights in North-East India,* Om Publication, New Delhi, p. 196.
6. Office File, *All Manipur Social Reformation and Development Samaj,* Imphal.
7. *Interviewed* with Smt. K. Taruni Devi, President, All Manipur Social Reformation and Development Samaj.
8. Zehol, T.V. Lucy, 1988, Women's Movement in Manipur: Some Observations, in Karna, M.N. (Ed.), *Movements in North-East India,* Indus Publishing Company, New Delhi, p. 72.
9. *Times of India,* dt. 20.08.2014, p. 1.

7
Globalization and Women Empowerment

Globalization is a process of ever-growing economic interdependence of countries of the world which constitutes integration of national economies into the international economy through cross-border transactions in goods and services, international capital flows and widespread diffusion of technology. Globalization allows the access to ideas and international best practices in different fields and realms—a new production technology, a new managerial practice, it can even be a certain set of institutions that has proved successful in other places, and eventually, a model of society. As globalization is often associated with increased instability of output and employment, this affects, among other things—job security. Globalization does not only mean the inter-relationship, inter-dependent and inter-connectivity of markets and productions of the different parts of the globe due to the dynamics of trade in goods and services and flows of capital and technology. It includes all aspects of human life of which economy is only a part. It enhances the inter-connectivity among States mediated by new communication technology transcending the existing organizational administrative and legal boundaries. The States have little choice, but to actively cooperate and collaborate with one another, resulting in what is known as crises. Global inter-connectedness has reduced border controls which earlier served to restrict transactions in goods and services, production factors and technology, ideas and cultural exchange.[1]

Globalization has both positive and negative potentials as well as dangerous consequences which threatened the whole world. Positively, it avails the scientific, technological, medical and other innovations, though inadequate, in different facets of human development, involving level of living, employment and ways, literacy and education, nutrition and health. The negative consequences of globalization are suffered mainly by the marginalized group of people, i.e. growing unemployment due to inability of smaller industries to compete with the inter-national firms, loss of livelihood for traditional artisans and craftsmen, and migration of people for jobs and livelihood. As globalization takes the whole world as a single market, labour is losing its voice, National Governments are losing their powers and due to privatization, there is loss of guaranteed employment, which is the common feature all over the world. Globalization has led to elimination of women from industrial work.[2]

The ideological aspect of globalization is what has been called triumph of liberalism/capitalism. Lack of an alternative to liberalism gives rise to the view that capitalism is an inevitable world-wide phenomenon. With the collapse of socialist power and policies (Glasnost and Perestroika) as a serious alternative to capitalism, the opportunity of the non-Western world took the advantages. Inter-national organizations like World Bank and IMF force national governance into structural adjustment and deregulation, opening up these countries for Western products and capitals. It is being claimed that under globalization, with greater and multi-dimensional freedom and reliance on market mechanism, would result into empowerment of women, but when examined in deep the situation seems otherwise. The tension of globalization lies in its social effects. It leads to homogenization of culture in some significant aspects throughout the world. It does not, however, imply that the nature of reciprocity in global relationship is entirely equilateral, the inequalities based on capital, technological, power and human resources remain. Globalization has led to elimination of women from industrial work. Many a time, the contribution of women is neither given due attention nor marginalized while formulating socio-economic development plans. Being characterized by tradition of sex discrimination and social stratification, the Indian women also occupy a place of subordination to men in many occasions. But they shares distinct and equal footsteps along with the men folk of the society. In maximum societies, women had been considered naturally unsuited to political activity and had been formally or informally excluded from it. The legacy of this old belief, reinforced by unequal domestic division of labour not only handicaps women in the pursuit of political office, but also prevent them from being active in political participation of any type of nature. Women need protection of their rights and interests. Male alone should not make laws pertaining to the rights of women. Their active participation in law-making is of vital importance as there are good reasons to believe that issues affecting women are not given adequate scope in public life.[3] Many factories, which are based on primary sectors dominated by women labour, are in the process of winding up and large industrial global products made the products in small units redundant. This changing process is a big horror to the female workforce by eliminating their contribution in the labour markets. This wave of elimination of women from the workplace is also seen in the North-East States, especially in Manipur, although these States are not industrially strong. Modern industrial upsurge and economic reforms have proved discriminatory against women. A fallout of this economic and industrial transformation is the increase in violence against women as it gave a direct impact to the economic liberty of the womenfolk.

Women continue to perform expressive gender roles as housewives, nurturer of children and various domestic chores at home. Home is separated from workplace and women labour goes unpaid. Under prevailing framework of dominant economic norms women's domestic labour does not get any recognition. The division of labour in domestic chores and childcare is rarely renegotiated across the genders. Despite their increased labour input into paid work, women, particularly married women, either continued to bear the main burden of domestic work, or share it with other female members of the household, often their daughters. By and large, gender inequalities in work burdens appear to be intensified. After 1991, the Indian economy was opened up suddenly without the required economic and social policies to provide the required safety net to women. In India, generally and in Manipur particularly, due to the existing gender gap, women require Governmental support for their social and economic upliftment and empowerment. While a trend towards equalization of wages between men and women has been visible in the organized sector, discrimination in various ways is in throughout agriculture and the rest, the unorganized sector. Since 94 per cent of women workers are engaged in the unorganized sector they are unaffected by the protection afforded by the Labour Laws, and are victims of the low productivity, unemployment, abject poverty and exploitation by intermediaries. The women of India in general and Manipuri women in particular are well known for their hardworking nature. They are expert weavers and farmers in addition to being the carrier of their rich cultural heritage. But still they have also encounter some specific problems over ages such as—patriarchal culture, inadequate access to productive resources, non-accounting of household work, insufficient advancement, powerlessness etc.

Comparing the present state of women's economic participation to the situation prevailing in the traditional Indian economy, the Committee on the Status of Women in India observed that while women had played distinctive and accepted role in the process of production and exchange in the traditional economy as cultivators, artisans, traders and professionals, and continue to do so in those parts of the economy where traditional forms of economic organizations still prevail. The impact of transition to a modern economy has meant exclusion of an increasing number and proportion of women from active participation in the productive process.

A considerable number continue to participate fully are on sufferance, without equal treatment, security of employment and human conditions of work. A very large number of them are subjected to exploitation of various kinds with no protection from society or the State. In agrarian societies, the family being the unit of production and the place of work being close to the home, participation in the production process in both agriculture and industry is a family affair. Markets are mostly local or within accessible distance—giving women the opportunity to play an important role in the process of exchange, ensuring for them considerable economic independence. The movement from the traditional to a modern economy, which substitutes family labour by the competitive labour between individuals, invariably result in a decline in women's participation and the emergence of social theories relegating women to childcare and housework as their sole occupation. The following table shows the work participation rate of North-Eastern States of India after 1991.

Table 7.1: Work Participation Rate in North-East India

States	*Year*	*Male*	*Female*
Assam	1991	49.45	21.61
	2001	49.93	20.80
Arunachal Pradesh	1991	53.76	37.49
	2001	50.69	36.45
Manipur	1991	45.27	48.91
	2001	48.91	40.51
Meghalaya	1991	50.07	34.93
	2001	47.76	35.02
Mizoram	1991	53.87	43.52
	2001	57.45	47.63
Nagaland	1991	46.86	37.96
	2001	46.82	38.25
Tripura	1991	47.55	13.76
	2001	50.81	21.02

Source: Census Report of India.

Development, urbanization and population growth have inevitably changed the traditional base of the economic activities of the modern women. Many avenues are opening up beyond the activities of the farm, handloom and handicraft\s and marketing of home products. But the crisis is that, work available in the traditional sectors is not expanding and new works available in the urban and rural sectors are far short of the rising women's labour force. The result has been the absolute marginalization of female workforce. Women, mainly poor, rural and lower class that had been in the forefront of production activities are desperately searching for work in unproductive activities to eke out a living and feed her children. The economic and social impact of marginalization and slow growth of employment has been most severely felt by the women folk of the whole workforce. These women folks who are unemployed most of the year are the ones that one sees flooding the sandy by lanes, the pavement of market towns, in the kitchens of the middle class, stone and sand quarries, construction works, *pan dukans,* clinics, parlours, hotels, vegetable vendors, maidservants, daily labour etc. Those who are not lucky enough to find even these low end employment or do not have the source of capital to ply a trade, have found their way into the fast growing profession of prostitution or sex worker.[4] The increasing commercialization and growing consumerism have opened still new avenues for sexual exploitation of women. Like all other commodities women have also become a 'commodity'. Advertising industry and sales promotion mechanisms fully exploit the bodily/physical charm of women. Not only the body, but its different parts are used to give 'special effect'. From lips to legs almost every organ becomes a means to tempt consumers. Another fact of globalization is the increasing tourist traffic which has also added a new dimension to women's sexual exploitation. Tourism is now developing into an industry and it is a very lucrative proposition for various tourist agencies as well as foreign exchange earner to the Government in developing countries. As part of promoting tourism, women are being increasingly used as sex workers. In Manipur the term 'sex worker' and 'prostitutes' are so odd and uncommon. But as per record of an NGO, MAC expressed that there are 260-270 sex workers at Moreh only. Out of which 160-170 are Myanmarese.[5]

Thus, women though hard work and expert in many fields, are still a subjugated and dominated social group. Still they have also encountered some specific problems over ages such as—patriarchal culture, inadequate access to productive resources, non-accounting of household works, insufficient advancement facilities, powerlessness etc. Consequently, women are commodified, made chief labours and are made instrumental enhancing the market for commodities. Atrocities on women at their working places, as well as, outside, which have resulted in rape, molestation including murder cited as instances of exploitation, oppression and subjugation of women. Rape of female patients by doctors and sexual torture of women in police custody are not unknown in this country. Trafficking, sexual abuses, violence against women and many other crimes like these are increasing day-by-day. Media are so alert regarding the information of the steps taken up by the Government for the prevention of the crimes against women and steps for development of women. At the same time the news of the violence against women, including the minor, is also increasing. Food and health care is another domain where women are discriminated against men due to their economic position. It is advanced that women and the girl child are always neglected in this respect. It is abject poverty and deprivation that lie at the root of the problem and not the supposed discriminatory attitude. Except few lucky employees of Central and State Governments and/private organizations, millions of women and girl-child belonging to lower and lower middle classes in India are left to their fate when they fall sick or suffer from serious ailments. Those who can manage and are economically well of do not make any distinction between boys and girls. But the fact remains that when the bread winner of a poor and lower middle class family suffers he is given more attention than females and girl child under similar circumstances.[6] These are the main causal factors for the problems of women empowerment.

It is quite clear that man-woman relation is ordained by nature, and power structure is imposed by the social codes and behaviour inherited by them. The economic structures mainly determined this power relation within the family as well as in the society. This is true both in the capitalist and traditional primitive productive system. Subsistence farming, hunting, grazing and forestry inevitably kept the women at the back seat of power structure. But without these activities poor rural families will be difficult to sustain their life. Women, who are belonging to the urban educated middle class are something aware of their health, empowerment etc. even though that cannot be compared with the male members. But the poor rural uneducated women are not bothering about their health, nutrition, empowerment etc. In spite of their status or empowerment or value, they do not hesitate to work in the agricultural farms, hard manual works, carpenter, pot making etc. along with the men. They do not have any choice of work on the bases of their health or work place and only their concern is to earn money and feed the family. But in such societies men never are ready to do work of household chores, and always maintain the division of labour on the bases of gender.

In Manipur, as belonging to the poor underdeveloped society and due to the existing gender inequalities under the strict patriarchal social structure, women require active governmental support for their socio-economic upliftment and empowerment. If they are not empowered and developed, the society cannot be regarded as a developed society because they

Table 7.2: Changing Sex-Ratio since 1951 in North-East India

States	*1951*	*1961*	*1971*	*1981*	*1991*	*2001*	*2011*
Assam	868	869	896	910	923	932	—
Arunachal Pradesh	—	894	861	862	859	901	—
Manipur	1036	1015	980	971	958	958	987
Meghalaya	949	937	942	954	955	975	—
Mizoram	1041	1009	946	919	921	938	—
Nagaland	999	933	871	868	886	909	—
Tripura	904	932	943	946	945	950	—

Source: Census Report 2011.

constitute 49.67 per cent of the total population of Manipur. Since 1951, the female sex ratio is declining in Manipur, Mizoram, and Nagaland, and slightly in Meghalaya, even though the remaining three States in North-East India are improving.

The attention of export oriented manufacturing and agriculture should not detract attention from an important fact of life. The North-East region of India was well known for its self-sufficiency and its rich natural resources. Up to 1962 Census Manipur had enough food production of its own. The natural resources of the region were harnessed sustainably by the indigenous people, but mainly by the women in the tribal areas. After the liberalization of the economy and in the new circumstances created by SAP for globalization, the traditional role of women is being undermined whereas mechanization and automation is becoming prevalent in the market based economy which has adversely affected the village based traditional economy. The opening of markets led to the commercialization of agriculture and new technologies penetrated into our agricultural lands. But in this context too regarding upgradation of agricultural development tools women were neglected. The transmission of knowledge about the new technologies like use of tractors, high quality fertilizers, selection of HYV seeds, pesticides etc. became man-to-man affairs. Men were increasingly drawn into the modernizing agriculture sector while women stayed in subsistence agriculture with no access to credits, training and technologies. The agricultural development has normally and almost entirely been manned by men right from the decision-making to implementation.[7]

Socially and culturally women are still tradition bound and it is a disadvantageous position. They are well known for their hardworking nature-expert weavers and farmers, in addition to being the career of rich culture. After globalization, the traditional work culture and role of women is being undermine whereas mechanization and automation is prevailing in the market based economy which has adversely affected the village based traditional economy. With the advent of globalization, the same works which were women's exclusive domain came to be undertaken by men and machines, and women's works which determined their identity were snatched away reduced women to mere consumers rather than producers. Economic independence or access to an inherited or self-generated income is considered to be the major means of empowering women. Thus, women are still a subjugated and dominated social group instead of emancipation and empowerment. Being influenced by unique physical, racial and socio-cultural diversities quite different from the rest of the country, North-East India witnesses a great variation in socio-economic conditions of women in both spatial and social terms. It is obvious that discrimination exists. Women do not have the opportunities that men do. And women that do not conform to the system, who try to break with the accepted patterns, are stigmatized as 'odds' and 'unfeminine'.

But one of the biggest responsibilities of the empowered women today is how to synthesize what has been valuable and timeless in our ancient traditions with what is good and valuable and timeless in our ancient traditions with what is good and valuable in modern thought. Women are assets who can reshape and reconstruct the society in all aspects such as socially, economically, politically, academically and so on. So, women should be empowered with greater access to knowledge and resources, greater autonomy in decision-making to enable them to have greater ability to plan their lives or have greater control over the circumstances that influence their lives and free from shackles imposed on them by customs, beliefs and practices.

Although women may have many interests in common, the fabric of their lives and the choices available to them may vary widely, but still it is in the hands of men. Now, for India to become what we want it to become with a modern, rational society and firmly based on what is good in our ancient tradition and in our soil, for this we have a thinking public, thinking young women who are not content to accept what comes from any part of the world, but are willing to listen to it, to analyze it and to decide whether it is to be accepted or whether it is dethrone out and this is the sort of empowerment which we want, which enables our young people to adjust to this changing world and to be able to contribute to it. If not the meaning of new global liberal economy will fail in this context. Making any good policy will have its meaning only when it is applicable and benefited to all the people.

The women empowerment is the ability of women to exercise power and knowledge for betterment of life and society. It is to do with getting and sharing the power; and remaining, exercising and controlling power leading to democratic system and inclusive growth. The primary goal for women empowerment is to improve the quality of life of women, yet it has also deep ramification in social, economic and political scenario. Economic independence is the yardstick of emancipation and empowerment which gives them self-confidence and the decision-making power. If women are economically independent at least their voice is heard if not heeded. Empowerment is not something which can be made in capsule form for those whom we think is in need of it. It is not just a concept that could be defined with the help of some universally accepted parameters. Empowerment is a process and includes the following components: Equal access to opportunities for using society's resources; Prohibition of gender discrimination in thought and practice; Freedom from violence; Economic independence; Participation in all decision-making bodies; and Freedom of choice in matters relating to one's life.[8]

United Nations declared 25th November as the "International Day for Elimination of Violence against Women." And, the year 2001 was declared as the "International Women's Empowerment Year" by the United Nations. Simultaneously, the Government of India also declared the same year as "Women Empowerment Year." Empowerment of women is essentially a broader concept heralding a shift from unjust to just, subservient to successful, passive to active womenhood. It refers to reversing gender base social, economic and political inequalities. It involves a complex interplay of various factors like physical, social, economic, political, psychological and attitudinal.

In North-East India, mainly in the tribal societies even after the introduction of Right to Property Act, 2005, women do not have land ownership, but they are engaged in cultivation, doing all the pre-harvest and post-harvest works. We, therefore, find that in the turn of new millennium women's position in the different walks of life would remain at the low level. In agriculture, women are workers giving only their labour, but they have no decision-making power in various activities. The decision-making power of women is limited, since they do not have earning power. Even where they are earner, their decision-making power in the household are compromised and curtailed as their outside activities are limited. This is the general feature of women's status in the country. The rhetoric of empowerment is enabling women to become victims of oppressors who should be brought to book. Our judges and lawyers, the police and the criminal justice system in most of the cases fail to give justice to women victims, and the offenders are acquitted most of the time. Policy and its implementation have made many prescriptions in different directions. Many new responsibilities have been added without any reduction in the basic set of deprivations of work burdens; employment and education are becoming tools for family welfare. Ideally, these should have been women's source of freedom; birth control is manipulating for population control rather than relieving women from reproductive burdens.

Economic empowerment of women is the prerequisite for family and societal conditions. Earning opportunities of women have to be ensured in different sectors. The Government has to extend and develop multiple productive and employment opportunities. Training of women and technological adaptation are important for transmission of productive capabilities of the women. In the spheres of social and household relations the important task for women empowerment is to raise the social awareness by continuous exhortation. Every person in the society and in the family has to be aware of the right, needs, well and woes, pleasure and pain as well as honour and dignity of the women. Apart from economic power, the enlightened and intelligent family members must have a balanced view in the family decisions. Very often material greed of the family lead to harassment of women. The enlightenment and education are important to fight against this repression.[9]

Literacy in India is key for socio-economic progress and the Indian literacy rate grew to 74.04 per cent in 2011 from 12 per cent at the end of British rule in 1947. Although this was a greater than six-fold improvement, the average level of schooling of women labour force is still less than primary level. Researcher in the area have brought out that such low level human capital are fundamentally inadequate for sustained development and poverty eradication. It has also pointed out that without schooling, the development goals cannot be achieved. The role of education in reducing poverty and inequality has been strongly established. Illiteracy is one of the strongest predictors of poverty and unequal access to educational opportunity is one of the income inequalities between male and female. It is clearly visible in societies, in respect of girls and people living in rural areas. Extending adequate quality education to the women is crucial to equip them to contribute to and benefit from economic growth. Despite decades of development the fact remains that women are a deprived section of society. No law of the country is against the women, but due to the unfavourable social factors women are discriminated. Due to the traditional as well as the prevailing social conditions women are having such unbearable problems. Not only the benefits of development have eluded women as a category, in some way development processes have enhanced male domination over women and added to their deprivation. As well as they cannot except from the household chores. Unpaid twenty-four hours multi-tasking of the women are not known by the society. Opportunities and reservations for education have increased, but the rate of female literacy and enrolment in educational institution is much less than men in Indian scenario. Even though the female literacy rate of some States of North-East India are higher than the national average (74.08%—Female 65.46 and male 82.14), it cannot be translated into higher emplloyability or productivity because of the slow

Table 7.3: Literacy Rate of North-East India since 1981

States	*Year*	*Male*	*Female*
Assam	2001	71.93	56.03
	1991	61.87	43.03
	1981*		
Arunachal Pradesh	2001	64.07	44.24
	1991	51.45	29.69
	1981	35.12	14.02
Manipur	2011	86.49	73.17
	2001	77.87	59.70
	1991	71.63	47.60
	1981	64.15	34.67
Mizoram	2001	90.64	86.13
	1991	85.61	78.60
	1981	79.36	86.13
Nagaland	2001	71.77	61.92
	1991	67.62	54.75
	1981	58.58	41.39
Tripura	2001	61.49	65.41
	1991	70.58	49.65
	1981	81.47	65.41

* No census was done for Assam due to Anti-foreigner Agitation.
Source: Census Report of India 2011.

pace of industrialization and limited capacity of the population to engage in productive economic activities. It means unemployment and underemployment.

Women are vital part of Indian economy, constituting one-third of the national labour force and major contributor to the survival of the family. Women are builders of the nation right from early days in their homes and it is at their hands that the children received their first education. Micro-economic research has revealed that education improves individual incomes. Research also indicates the contribution of education to better natural resource management and more rapid technology adaptation and innovation. When a large share of women do not complete education, the productivity of the labour force and the women potential from which the society and economy can draw, are limited. In several developing regions, the average level of schooling of women labour force is still less than primary level. Researchers in the area have brought out that such low level human capital are fundamentally inadequate for sustained development and poverty eradication. It has also been pointed out that without schooling, the development goals cannot be achieved. The role of education in reducing poverty and inequality has been strongly established. Illiteracy is one of the strongest predictors of poverty and unequal access to educational opportunity is one of the income inequalities. It is clearly visible in societies, in respect of girls and people living in rural areas. Extending adequate quality education to the women is crucial to equip them to contribute to and benefit from economic growth.

Conclusion

Globalization is certainly converting the world into a single global village, but it has failed to weed out the inequalities in society in various aspects of life. This has brought the people closer, but widens the gap between power and powerlessness, have and have not, rich and poor. The world today needs a human process of globalization such that the global disparities are not there.

The new economic reforms after 1991 should have to be studied with the advantages and disadvantages of women. If their status and problems are not looking after with reference to different changes in the policies and programmes of the Government, it will be very late for solving the overall problems of the society because they are taking a key role in the process for the development of the society as a whole. Most are still struggling with disease and death, because of inadequate sanitation, improper guidance and the lack of basic amenities for health and hygiene. It is time to ensure that every women has a hygienic, health and happy life, as their life. To this end, we support UNISEF with an aim to make a difference where it really matters. But this is not a task we can do alone. We need to come together, because women and men together can change another women's life and can make other women equal to her. Serious attention and a fresh looks are required to reorient our developmental model and policies, so that, economic development and women's development do not work at cross purposes. A concerted attempt has to be made to evolve strategies for the economic independence and socio-political empowerment of the majority of poor and illiterate women in both rural and urban areas. In the spheres of social and household relations the important task is to raise the social awareness by continuous exhortation. Every person in the society and in the family has to be aware of the rights, needs, well and woes, pleasure and pain as well as honour and dignity of the women. Women, in the position of making development, would also help to bring about change in attitude, beliefs and thoughts and in enhancing motivation and self-confidence among them. In the social life the bias against women and girl child has to be fought by social movements and by ensuring freedom to women from the oppressive social codes. Both men and women will have to work together in this direction, so that, human resources are not wasted or exploited by the brutal forces with the advent of globalization, the super national bodies like UN, EU, NAFTA, ASEA, APEC, IMF, World Bank and WTO will formulate policies and lay conditions like reductions of expenditure in social sectors, cut down in employment, government subsidies etc. are not necessarily acceptable to the weaker section of the society, i.e. women and poor will be victim of the situation. It is agreed that India does have a world class business community. But unless the State is transformed from a callous exploiter into one that actually serves citizens, unless we get a half satisfactory police-judicial system, unless we create incentives that reward desirable behaviour of officials and politicians and penalize undesirable behaviour, it will be difficult for Indian Government to interpret the real meaning of liberalization, privatization and globalization. Under the circumstances it can be upheld by ensuring women's empowerment, and realizing that women play a crucial role in the development of society, many underlying issues which lead to conflict and problems can be tackled more effectively. If not the situation of conflict and problems will increase and its resultant effect will suffer by the whole society.

Notes

1. Sengupta, Surojit, 2008, Globalization and its Impact on Society—Some Reflections; in Dev, B.J.; Sengupta, Keya, Ray, B. Dutta (eds.), *Globalization and North-East India,* Concept Publishing Company Pvt. Ltd., New Delhi, p. 157.
2. Krishan, Kewal and Th. Binarani Devi, 2014, Globalization and Women in North and North-East India: A Critical Study, *Journal of International Academic Research for Multidisciplinary,* Vol. 2, Issue 1, Febuary, pp. 146-47.
3. Borah, Anjan Jyoti, 2008, Literacy, Education and Political Participation of Women in Meghalaya: With Special Referance to Garo Hills—A Study, in Gassah, L.S. (ed.), *Women Empowerment Movement in North-East India,* Omson Publication, New Delhi, p. 124.
4. Krishan, Kewal and Th. Binarani Devi, *op. cit.,* p. 152.
5. *Sangai Express,* Imphal Daily Local Paper, p. 6, dated 15.12.2009.
6. Mao Xaveir P., 2008, Men *verses* Women—A Critique of Emancipative Ideology, in Gassah, L.S. (ed.), *Women Empowerment Movement in North-East India,* Omson Publication, New Delhi, p. 196.
7. Phukan, Dolly, 2008, New Economic Policy and Its Impact on Traditional Skills of Women in North-East India, in Dev, B.J.; Sengupta, Keya; Ray, B. Dutta (eds.), *Globalization and North-East India,* Concept Publishing Company Pvt. Ltd., New Delhi, p. 349.
8. Krishan Kewal, 2012, Legal Empowerment of Women at Work Place—Protective Measures, in *Indian Journal of Development Research,* Vol. 4, No. 3, July-August, p. 97.
9. Banerjee, Amalesh, 2006, Women Empowerment and Development, in Ray, B. Dutta and Ray, Asok Kumar (eds.), *Dynamics of Power Relations in Tribal Societies of North-East India,* Om Publications, New Delhi, pp. 130-31.

8

Liberal Economy, Women and Corporate Social Responsibility

India adopted the New Economic Policy in 1991 with an objective of integrating the Indian economy with the global economy. This new policy of liberalization, privatization and globalization was targeted to attract foreign investment, portfolio investment, multinational and transnational companies, simply it means opened in all directions with an interest quick development. Some foreign capital inflow surged in demanding immediate deregularisation of industry and trade, liberal exchange rate regime and drastic reduction of State economic activities by privatizing public enterprises. Foreign/Multinational Companies and investors intrude into the Indian Economic scenario with different principles of corporate social responsibility even before 1991, which contained different hopes and promises in favour of socio-economic development of India. But as a matter of fact, the condition of Indian economy with this New Economic Policy is economic growth without economic development for some regions and some states. These changing scenarios in the economic system and structure make a change in the indigenous culture, custom, moral and practices of the people in India. The opening of market economy led to commercialization of agriculture and new technology penetrated in the traditional fields and small scale industries. The condition is just survival of the fittest. The poor, backward and marginalized groups, especially women are pushed aside. The traditional skills of women in the agriculture, weaving etc. are being adversely affected. Working class women shared with their middle class counterparts some elements of the gender division of labour, and had limited access to resources—land, cash or the value of their own labour; whether in production or reproduction. In this sense, the capitalist exploitation of women as wage-earners was parasitic on their gender subordination—at home and in the workplace. Women's participation in factory work broke down or modified some instruments of social oppression, but it generated and intensified other inequalities.[1]

Socially and culturally women are still tradition, bound while the Government introduced the modern economy and it is a disadvantageous position. They are well known for their hardworking nature—expert weavers and farmers, in addition to being the career of rich culture of their respective societies. In most societies, all over the globe, the main role of women is expected and confined to performing the household chores, child bearing and care of the entire family. In the rural agrarian set-up, these duties are further extended to work in the fields, cultivation, plantation, forestry and fishery, poultry, tending cattle, providing for food, fuel and fodder and little more skill jobs in the forms of weaving, dying, printing and household industry. For these twenty-four hours multi-tasking of the women, there are no wages nor is the work recognized as much important as that of a man. Home is separated from workplace and woman labour goes unpaid. Not only that, the work is stereotyped and related with the sex roles and developmental tasks of women. Women continue to perform expressive gender roles as housewives, nurturer of children and various domestic chores at home. Under prevailing framework of dominant economic norms women's domestic labour does not get any recognition. The division of labour in domestic chores and childcare is rarely renegotiated across the genders. Despite their increased labour input into paid work, women (particularly married women) either continued to bear the main burden of domestic work, or share it with other female members of the household, often their daughters. By and large, gender inequalities in work burdens appear to be intensified. Even though women typically slipped back into housework and anonymity each time the tide ebbed, the possibility of asserting themselves on a larger scale was engraved in their memories. For a limited number of educated young women, programmes of economic and social development undertaken during the Five Year Plans provided possibilities for employment and, to some extent, self-determination. Although the number of females counted in the decennial census as workers in fields, factories and handicrafts continued to shrink, opportunities multiplied for them in Government agencies, business offices, bank branches, telephone exchanges, schools at all levels, hospitals, airlines, newspaper offices. Rapid expansion of higher education brought into being a corps of thoughtful and articulate young women serving as Instructors and Professors in the Universities and Colleges all over the country. Simply more and more women are getting involved in career building in this modern liberalized society, but only few have been able to reach the position of decision-making level or to serve on governing boards and bodies that influence media policy. Even those few who are at that level are having different type of problems—professionally as well as socially. In law conflict is the common happening at this stage. Here, women plus women support system is also quite important. Bringing in more and more women into decision-making, programming, research and promoting women will undoubtedly progress the nation as the need of the hour.

Women need not to underestimate themselves. They are embodied with different skills. They need to expose their innate capacity and calibre. Small business enterprises, run by women, play an important role in the economic development. These enterprises, may be in informal economic sectors, are now being proposed as a way to achieve sustainable socio-economic development and eliminate poverty related with the concerned environment.

Impact of Globalization on Indian Economy and Corporate Social Responsibility

Under globalization, free economy demand removal of pervasive restraints on economic freedom. One of the most foci of institutional reform is, therefore, to seek and establish liberating institutions in the countries for investment and aids.[2] The prime concern of these aid givers and investors are not only to gain political and monetary benefits. So, they rushed for finding out their markets with different soft corner mottos like taking care of environmental issues, job opportunities, cultural ties etc. Those business organizations were considered good which could reap profit for its owner or the organizers. It means that business is dominated by selfishness and there is no place for ethics on it. In this situation, it is not only difficult, but impossible to run business successfully for the underdeveloped and developing countries. These conditions give direct and indirect threats to the Indian social scenario. Globalization is certainly converting the world into a single global village, but it has failed to weed out inequalities in society in various aspects of life. These have brought the people closer, but widen the gap between haves and have-nots, rich and poor. The world of today needs a human process of globalization such that the global disparities are not there.[3]

Economic reforms in the long-run, serve as a means for harnessing the vast underutilized resources of a State for accelerating GDP growth rate along with this changing process. The individual performance of a State in this direction depends largely on the State's ability to provide an environment conducive to the new economic policy. Thus, it is the economically advanced States having a growth in a friendly environment buttressed by well developed infrastructure that have been benefited most by the economic reforms. On the other hand, the States-where infrastructural development, are at the initial or pre-reform period, have failed to take advantage of the opportunities opened up by the economic reforms for taking their economies to a higher growth path. Based on the World Bank Report, Alic Sindzingre expressed that differentiation across States since the early 1990s reflects acceleration of growth in some States, but deceleration in others. High growth performers were a mixed group (rich States, e.g., Karnataka, Kerala and West Bengal). Growth slowed down in the richer North-Western States of Haryana and Punjab because of the slowdown in agricultural growth. Growth stagnated in the States of Bihar, Odisha and Uttar Pradesh, which were initially poor.[4] The condition of North-East India is quite strange where the economy is mainly based on rural agriculture. The New Economic Policy has undoubtedly opened up the possibilities of harnessing immense potentials of the North-Eastern region for developmental imperatives which had hitherto remained illusive in the absence of economic infrastructure and strong political will. In India, as the industrial licensing policy has been withdrawn, the reform regime provides more room for State Government initiatives to attract industrial investments. As every State can take such initiatives, the States of North-East would have to compete with other States of India which are already advanced when it is compared with the backward North-Eastern States. There is the Central Government incentive packages for industrial location in the hilly North-Eastern region, but this does not help much because similar facilities has been extended to other Hill States, namely Himachal Pradesh and Uttarakhand.[5] The problem of ensuring equity in the distribution of the flow of benefits to different sections of population will remain as it was unless the problems of unemployment, poverty, food and health insecurities are directly tackled by implementing the employment guarantee scheme, and strengthening the public distribution system and anti-poverty programmes for providing social safety net for all sections of populations by the government along with the spontaneous cooperation and support of the general public. The problem is with those poor people, who belonged to the rural agriculturist section. While foreign countries and companies are searching for their destinations with full advertisement of corporate social responsibilities a problem arose with those of poor people, who belonged to the rural agriculturist section. The setting up of modern urbanized system had snatched away their humble means of livelihood and hence, could not afford or find it difficult. For example automobile companies are coming with the advertisement of pollution control, health care, less oil consumption, emergency services etc., but the primary concerned for these poor backward people is—food, cloth and shelter. Companies think that corporate social responsibility is a peripheral issue for their business and customers satisfaction more important for them. They imagine that customers' satisfaction is now only about price and service, but fail to point out an important change that are taking place worldwide that could blow the business out of the water.[6] The socio-economic conditions of these poor backward States of North-East lies in Gandhiji's idea "production by masses instead of mass production." This can be made possible through self-employment drive based on entrepreneurship development to a great extent.

Women Entrepreneurs and Act of Social Responsibility

Economic development of any country or any State is related with topography, climatic condition, soil, vegetation and many other natural phenomena. There is a need for proper arrangement of human and material resources. This can be done with entrepreneurship. Entrepreneurship is the most important determinant in the process of industrialization by covering all the length and breadth of any country. Entrepreneurship offers tremendous opportunities for women across the world by opening doors to greater self-sufficiency, self-esteem, education, and growth—not only for the women themselves, who are involving in the entrepreneurship, but also for their families and their employees. Economic independence or access to an inherited or self-generated income is considered to be the major means of empowering women. Full employment of a woman assures her a better, more enriching and rewarding life and human relationship. Entrepreneurship among women is a recent phenomenon. Therefore, it is desirable that first generation entrepreneurs with their limited financial resources and experiences should go in for small and rural industries. Today, we find women in different types of industries, traditional as well as non-traditional, from engineering and electronics to doll making and poultry.

Women entrepreneurs are individuals or group of women who initiate, organize and operate a business enterprise. Women entrepreneurs started their activities are mostly on their own initiatives to become self-sufficient and to establish their own identity. They are both individual and collective depending upon the situation. Though they come out from the traditional patriarchal power structures and taking up new roles and they can take decision of their own by creating something on their own efforts and view success by achieving their targets. Accordingly, the focus on economic development made women the subject rather than object of development and agents of changes rather than welfare recipient only. Women entrepreneurs not only generate immediate and large scale employment opportunities with relatively low investment, but also create a good sense of economic empowerment which is the foundation of the overall empowerment of women. They are trying to bring backward areas in the mainstream with national development, in other words, it is trying to bring a balance regional development by ensuring more equitable distribution of national income. The Government of India also introduced New industrial plans from time-to-time, e.g. ten years broad-based Industrial Policy – 1997 to 2007. As a result, the investment made due to the North-East Investment Policy of 1997 in the entire North-East region amounted to Rs. 1067 crore as against more than Rs. 20,000 crore in Haryana alone.[7] Unfortunately, again, not a single large scale industry came up in the entire North-East India where the existing infrastructures are not in favour of boosting up industries and markets. During the period from 2001 to 2005, as many as 19,940 small industries were closed down due to various reasons including lack of Government help[8]. Here, women who have often not been able to be considered as equal in the male controlled corporate structures have seen entrepreneurship as an appropriate and desirable means of livelihood. It facilitates the optimum utilization of locally available resources. Such business enterprises occupy an important position in planned development of Indian economy and have grown to be the most vital sector of our nation.

The most important contribution of women entrepreneurs to this present day society is that they are encouraging effective mobilization of country's untapped and unused resources. They are trying to show that business has not only economic obligation, it has social obligation too which is highlighted by the Company Act of 2013 (related with the control measures used by the Government to regulate the functions of the corporate sectors). Rural and local development is the primary concerned of the Gandhian principle of economic development based on *Sarvodaya* that is becoming so relevant for the economic development of developing countries like India. Section 135 and Schedule 7 of the Company Act, 2013 also clearly mentioned about the provision for a preference which should be given to the local area where a company operates. Schedule 7 clearly lists out the activities which a qualified company can take up in discharging its corporate social responsibility and includes promotion of education, promotion of gender equality and empowering women employment enhancing vocational skills.

Corporate social responsibility means the way in which business farms integrate environmental, economic and social concerns into their culture, values, strategy, decision-making and operation is an accountable and transparent manner and, therefore, leading to better practices in the business organizations[9]. With the idea of social obligation, women entrepreneurs imply the ideal of trusteeship in relation to accumulated wealth, talent of people, their outlook, social awareness and their earnings beyond their immediate needs which are again mentioned in the Company Act of 2013. Some entrepreneurs with talents have the ability to earn more than others. She would not cramp their intellectual, but would allow them to earn more. They adopt the attitude of trustees and use the bulk of their greater earnings for the good of the State. According to Gandhiji, trustees may get remuneration for the work done through common consent of workers and the State. There must be parity between the remuneration of the trustees and the workers and should normally not be more than the latter. The managerial skill of the trustees, the talent and expertise of labour was neither to be exploited nor used to sub-serve vested interests of the few. On the contrary, society as a whole must derive the benefits.[10] With the activities of the women entrepreneur it is exhibited that the organizers/ property owners should not consider themselves as the absolute lords of what they possess; instead they should regard themselves as the custodians of social wealth or trustees utilizing their property and talent in contributing for the good of the whole community. Apart from earning, they use even their talents for the good of the community. Women entrepreneurs make themselves available for consultation and advice as and when needed by others. For industrially backward districts and areas, they have also taken a number of promotional measures such as conducting techno-economic survey, establishment of Technical Consultancy Organizations (TCO), encouragement of Entrepreneurship Development Programme (EDP). Thus, they stand for socialization of property as well as prosperity.

Entry of women into business is a new phenomenon traced out as an extension of their kitchen activities generally known as 3Ps—pickle, powder and *pappad*. This type of large scale participation by women helps to improve not only the women's self-employment, but also helps to develop the national economy. The handloom and handicraft—small cottage industries, mostly operated by women are contributing handsomely in the growth of GDP and GNP. Overall, it is seen in that there is dearth of enthusiasm and zeal amongst women of today to compete in the international arena. With the advancement of science and technology, there have been tremendous changes in the life styles of men and women especially in urban areas. Due to development in education, transport, media, communication, changes in family life and sex mores, women's education and participation in the world of work in urban areas has gained impetus after Independence of our country. More and more women, year after year, are making a thrust in the vocations which were primarily male dominated merely four decades back. With the growing awareness about business and spread of education among women over the period, women have started shifting from 3Ps to 3Es—engineering, electronics and energy and other industries under Integrated Rural Development Programme. They have excelled also in these activities. The successful and accomplished women entrepreneurs like Ila Bhatt (social enterpreneur), Smt. Kiran Majumdar Shaw (bio-technology), Smt. Shahnaj Hussain (beauty clinic), Smt. Sumati Morarji (Shipping Corporation), Naina Lal Kidwai (banking) etc. proved beyond doubt that given the opportunities, they can excelled and compete with their male counterparts.

The women of North-East in general and Manipuri women in particular are well-known for their hardworking nature. They are expert weavers and farmers in addition to being the carrier of their rich cultural heritage. Women in North-East India, though hard work expert in many fields, are still a subjugated and dominated social group. Still the introduction of New Economic Policy did not seem to help or uplift the position of women in Manipur. The status of women remained low and even became more vulnerable in North-East India. So, a proper research study of differential impact of liberalization, privatization and globalization on different sections of women is quite necessary.

Entrepreneurship offers tremendous opportunities by opening doors to greater self-sufficiency, self-esteem, education, and growth for the development of the society. These enterprises, may be in informal economic sectors, are now being proposed as a way to achieve sustainable socio-economic development and eliminate poverty in North-East India from the grassroots level. The women entrepreneurs of this region are very artistic; they designed different types of products especially in the traditional and cultural based industrial products. There is high demand for these agro-based industrial products which could not be met by these locally run business groups, the volume of the business is low due to many difficulties faced by the local entrepreneurs. Most of the women enterprises are engaged mainly in traditional activities like weaving, handloom, handicraft, knitting, embroidery, fruit processing industry etc. However, in recent years it has been observed that women entrepreneurs are venturing into non-traditional activities like beauty parlours, zeroxing, incense stick making, restaurants etc.[11] This chapter is trying to justify by taking up two case studies of Manipur, a tiny border State in North-East India. One is a very low level earning, but doing at their best. Another one is one of the most successful renowned entrepreneurs of Manipur. They are working at two different levels, but running their entrepreneurs successfully at their own level respectively. They are none other than—Brightway SHG and KETWAN.

Brightway SHG: It was established on September 5, 2005 at Elangbam Leikai Leirak Achouba, under the leadership of Smt. Mayengbam Ranjana Devi, 45 years. It was started with minimum amount for minimum earning with the free time activities. Eighteen women jointly worked and produced spices, turmeric, chilly powder, *besan* etc. Their products are selling through female hawkers of the SHG to the local shops of different districts of Manipur, mainly at Khwairamband Bazar. As the products are pure and chemical free the products are highly in demands. Purchases are demanded especially for marriage and religious ceremonies. With the objectives of providing job opportunities to the local women to earn extra income for themselves while engaging them in different economic activities during free time, one difficulty is that their working hour is limited as they could not be engaged for long hours as the members are coming to the work after completing their household chores. If there is any extra contribution like high selling, high production etc. the beneficiary got some monetary award from the centre.[12]

KETAWN: It was established in 1980 at Yumnam Leikai Nambul Mapal, Imphal East with the financial support from NEDFI and private loan. The proprietor of the centre is Smt. Yumnam Sorajini Devi. At present 97 workers are working at this centre with a varied monthly income of Rs. 3500 to Rs. 15,000 per month. There is a fixed working hour, i.e. 8 hour per day. For encouraging the working skill and interest of the employees, they are giving yearly and festival bonus, performance bonus, medical benefits etc. Their products are quite typical. They produced modern as well as traditional items. With the modern techniques they produced different handloom and handicraft items based on the culture and tradition.

The main production of the centre are hand embroidery, appliqué, zari works, frame needle, zig-zag embroidery, computerized embroidery (first time in North-East) and sequins embroidery. KETAWN has its own showroom which enables direct customer interaction. If in case anybody among the employees wishes to develop their own skill and interest for establishing their own entrepreneur, the Proprietor of KETAWN gives guidance and provides small interest loans or subsidy, but the centre has no yet proper branch as such.

Not only to produce goods and selling, KETAWN gives training to other women who are interested in the field. During the last seven years, members of the centre imparted certain skill development training and programme with the beneficiaries of more than 3000 trainees under the sponsorship of the Minorities and Other Backward Classes (MOBC), Government of Manipur, Manipur Urban Development Agency (MUDA), C/o the Development Commissioner Handicraft, Ministry of Textile, Government of India[13].

Entrepreneurship is viewed as a critical activity to regenerate and sustain economic growth in strong economies and also as a means to boosting employment and productivity in depressed regions or in developing countries. The dynamic process of new firms introduces and dispenses innovative products, processes and organizational structures throughout the economy. As firms enter and exit the market, they suggest that the new arrivals will be more efficient than those they displace. Furthermore, existing firms that are not driven out are forced to innovate and become more productive to compete.[14]

Role of the Government for Strengthening Women Entrepreneurs

On the question of availability of raw materials, which is the major bottleneck in the rapid expansion of small scale unit production, the Eighth Plan observed, "in the case of critical raw materials, new enterprises face problems in obtaining these in the absence of a proper and equitable policy of raw material distribution. After the de-control of steel price, drying up of canalizing agencies, and the devaluation of the Rupee, the availability of raw materials, particularly to the small producer, has been severely affected."

The solution suggested by the Eighth Plan, to encourage Industry Association to evolve a suitable distribution mechanism of raw materials, to protect the interests of the small sector, is to say the least, a very undependable solution. It virtually amounts to leaving the allocation pattern to the dictates of the markets. But the market mechanism follows the rule of the jungles, which is 'survival of the fittest'. It is only with the help or the purposeful intervention of the society, that the survival of the weak or the unfitted small scale industries can be ensured. If civilization means, the survival of the weak, then the arm of the State must ensure, a policy of equitable distribution of raw materials, but the new economic policy which over bonds in favour of the market mechanism, cannot be trusted to protect the interest of the small scale industrial sectors.

The ongoing poverty alleviation programmes are expected to address specifically the needs and problems of such women as poverty affects women more than men. So, the Tenth Plan proposes to ensure provision of training, employment and income generation activities with both 'Forward' and 'Backward' linkages with the ultimate objectives of making all women economically independent and self-reliant through different programmes. Organizing women into self-help groups under various poverty alleviation programmes—(1) Swarnajayanti Gram Swarojgar Yojana, (2) Swarnajayanti Shahari Rojgar Yojana, (3) Rashtriya

Mahila Kosh, (4) Support for Training and Employment Programmes, (5) Training-*cum*-Production Centres for Women etc. and offering them a range of economic options along with necessary support measures to enhance their objective of making them economically independent and self-relevant.

There are other capacity-building schemes for women entrepreneurs like 'Stree Shakti', 'SEWA', 'Swayamsiddha' and 'Swadhara', which have been launched with the idea of social and economic empowerment of women by ensuring direct access to and control over resources through a process of mobilization and convergence.

Government also encouraged women entrepreneurs to enter into various small scale industries or entrepreneurs which are reflected in various policies and programmes launched by them, e.g. Prime Minister Rojgar Yojana. North-Eastern Development Finance Corporation Ltd. (NEDFI), established on August 1995, has some special scheme like Women Enterprises Development Schemes (WEDS) for the economic empowerment of women of North-East India. The Ministry of Development of North-Eastern Region (DONER), established in September 2001 and accorded the status of a full-fledged Ministry on May 2004 has been providing fund and finance management for improving the financial position of the State including the small scale industries.

Problem Faced by Women in Performing Socio-Economic Activities

Indian cultural practices played strong role in restricting development of women, on the other side. Both in urban and rural areas, women experience great many difficulties in their daily struggle for survival, even when they have established their own enterprises and earn money for their daily use. They are mostly categorized as hawkers and vendors, piece rated workers, petty producers and those provide consumer services among the class of people who are not able to pay high service charges for the same.

It is rather to note that the work structure for educated and uneducated, employed or unemployed women, have basic similarities in the domestic front. They have been intruding into the realm of work which men do, but they have not been leaving their household works like cooking, washing, cleaning etc. plus to serve their husband, kids and in-laws. In both cases, there is no reward, monetary or otherwise, for performing the household jobs, which are mainly indoors. It includes cooking, healthcare, cleaning, washing and shopping for food and fuel, and to look after the family. But outside the home, the work situation, and structure are hierarchically related to the level of education.

Women play a very useful role in the family and community as major contributors to family income both urban and rural areas with entrepreneurship (large and small). They ply a crucial role in agrarian economy as invisible contributors to production process. During the off seasons, most of them are engaged in some kind of home-based production or micro-business and are victims of harse working conditions and go through series of economic problems, with no legal protections. The social legislations at the grassroots are totally ineffective. Rampant alcoholism, using of intoxicated drug, gambling etc. among men results in low male contribution in the family. They not only avoid their duties, are giving problems to the household affairs.

Not only the social problems, there are a lot of technical problems in connection with the activities of the women entrepreneurs. The production process in the small scale industries are greatly affected by lack of proper infrastructural facilities. Band, blockade, lack of water supply, good roads, medical facilities, sanitation etc. also hampered the production process. Therefore, there is an urgent necessity to address this problem. Production processes in small scale industries suffer badly for want of adequate and unfailing supply of power. Frequent power cuts and load shedding have affected the sector badly. Electricity is one of the biggest issues faced by the entrepreneurs. Even the productions are not depending upon electricity, the workers need light for other purposes.

Non-availability of funds, coupled with raw materials, is one of the major problems of the small scale industries. Moreover, low labour productivity, coupled with problems of labour unrest, add to the woes of the small scale industrial units. If the small sector should move into progress rapidly both in modernization and diversification of production efforts should be made to improve the level of technology, by producing sophisticated machines within the country.

With the introduction of developmental measures, the production relations have been modified and distribution system is being influenced by the market forces. Thus, the situation has undergone sea-change since Independence with the gradual transformation of the economy from the non-monetized to the market economy and the integration of the indigenous people in the national 'mainstream'. But starting and operating a business involves considerable risk and effort, because the entrepreneurs create and build everything on their own and assume all the responsibilities. Moreover, this risk is perhaps even greater for a woman entrepreneur, who has all the usual business problems as well as the problems associated with being a women in male dominated society. In spite of this, increasing number of women are entering into the business world and starting and operating their own business. Women perform most of the work in the family, but they are also taking active part in business and setting up their own enterprises. In Manipur women entrepreneurs are of any age group, i.e. starting from young age like 20s and even 70s too. They are taking some new roles which are productive in nature, and which will also give them to establish their own identity, and again they are competitive to each other in all fields for the success of their business. Most of them were first generation entrepreneurs who have started their business on their own initiatives.

Not only the point that both rural as well as urban female labour, but also that the lower and higher caste females respond favourably to labour market conditions, if a specific socio-economic and historic environment becomes conducive to entry in the job market, is relevant. In general, the female labour market depends not only on good economic opportunities, but also on the kind of occupational avenues which are available for females. Given the biological and social construction of gender roles, women tend to concentrate in jobs where they can combine their household duties and 'work'. Thus, cottage and construction industries provide them with 'appropriate' chances. Interestingly enough, even, the recent changes in the labour market, i.e. increasing contractual labour—essentially females and children working at home for the factory-based producers—seem to subscribe to the traditional order. The additional advantage is, of course, the fact that such labour is cheap and easily exploitable on various counts. This is true of all the countries across the subcontinent although the exact manner and degree to which this happens varies a great deal.

Value of Women for Socio-economic Development

Women are the beginning of everything. On her side, she needs to understand everything, aware of all the consequences, be able to fight and challenge all those obstacles, to acquire all the knowledge in all around her all the time. But without empowerment, the above mentioned conditions are impossible. Women are assets who can reshape and reconstruct the society in all aspects such as socially, economically, politically, academically and so on. So, women should be empowered with greater assess to knowledge and resources, greater autonomy in decision-making to enable them to have greater ability to plan their lives or have greater control over the circumstances that influence their lives and free from shackles imposed on them by customs, beliefs and practices. Power can, simply be defined as control over resources and control of ideology and understanding and it is exercised through a series of orders or decision-making capacity. Empowerment does not mean competition with men; in fact empowering women will enable them to eradicate all kinds of ignorance. They can participate in all kinds of activities and cooperate with men to bring about or more sociably and natural environment, e.g. in the field of literacy, health, social, economic, political, public administration, legal, local, global environmental issues, industrial, science and technology etc. From this point, empowerment is an active, multidimensional process which should enable women to realize full identity and powers in all spheres of life. It would consist of greater access to knowledge and resources, greater autonomy in decision-making, greater ability to plan their lives, greater control over the circumstances that influence lives and free them by customs, beliefs and practices.[15]

Women tend to be the primary care givers for children and elders. Their careers tend to be viewed as secondary to that of their spouses. But with the advancement of education and modernization women are exhibiting their outstanding role and contributions in all fields. So, if society recognized their role and contributions, the progress of the society will be more quickened. In this regard, I accept Arun Duggle's mentorship programme that aims to increase the presence of women on corporate boards. If they are included in the decision-making process and action on society and environment, through the transparent and ethical behaviour that is consistent inclusive and sustainable development, we can get the exact obligation of the corporate social responsibility, because they experienced the social reality. Here, women plus women support system is quite necessary. Women face a lot of pressures coming from the environment, at traditional (social) mindset and they are very difficult to come out from this social segregation of women from leadership strata. The absence of amenities for childcare extended women's responsibilities. Many women rushed in and out of the factory to feed or care for babies. This was not conducive to a commitment to the workplace. Women tended to depend greatly on support of other women—but such networks of support were based as much on neighbourhood and kin, as on relations developed in the workplace. Women who received help in housework did so in most cases from daughters, mothers and other female relatives.[16] When Aruna Jayenthi, CEO Capgemini India, got married, her mother-in-law introduced her to their neighbouring friends. The striking question from the neighbour was *"Abhi tak tumne naukri nahi chhora*? (You have not left your job.) Aruna Jayenthi with full personality of a leader made no answer, but tried to overcome these social challenges. Aruna Jayenthi introduced a coaching and mentoring programme last year for women in Capgemini India. There was first a coaching programme of three four months for mentors. And then the mentors were assigned to high potential women. One of the objectives of the programme is to see that the women do not drop out of work. The women are also given roles they are comfortable with.[17] Women in India are moving to love, sex (or *vice versa*) and then, may be marriage. It is not exactly mean that this is the main reason behind divorce, though it is certainly part of it. The primary reason is the financial independence of Indian women. They are now focusing more on their careers than on their personal lives. Not that they have it easy. Indian women are dealing with new and more Western problems such as career goals, sex, money while also dealing with traditional problems of overbearing mother-in-laws, child rearing etc. this puts way too much pressure on relationships. A big eye opener was the fact that caste is no longer the be-all and end-all of marriage now-a-days. Profession, education and money are more important.

The women entrepreneurs implemented the corporate social responsibility model beyond compliance and engaged in action that appears to further some social good, especially for women. Self-directly and for the society as a whole indirectly, beyond the interest of the firm and that which is required by law. Corporate social responsibility is a process with the aim to embrace responsibility for the company's actions and encourage a positive impact through its activities on the environment, consumer employees, communities, stakeholders and all other members of the public spheres who may also be considered as stakeholders. Proponents argue that corporate make more long-term profits by operating with a perspective while critics argue that corporate social responsibility distracts from the economic role of business. Corporate social responsibility has neutral impact on financial outcomes. Some argue that corporate social responsibility is merely window dressing or an attempt to pre-empt the role of government as a watchdog over powerful multinational corporations. The society provides infrastructure facilities for smooth working of a commercial organization and in turn expects the commercial organization to accept certain social responsibilities, so that, both the society and the organization are benefited.[18] The business is now required to watch the interest of its stakeholders, viz. employees, consumers, shareholders, general public and the government. The traditional objective of profit maximization is no longer valid so long as the primary utility of a business entity as representing and safeguarding the interests is well taken care of.

Conclusion

Development cannot take place unless the people at the grassroots level are not involved in the development programme. According to the modern point of view the objectives of business is to discharge its moral responsibility towards all the parties concerned and also earn profits simultaneously. The emerging concept for the need of social responsibility of the business corporate are due to the fact that—business is a part of society, avoidance of Government regulations, long-term self-interest business etc. Development business ethics is one of the forms of applied ethics that examines ethical principles and moral or ethical problems that can arise in a business environment. So, today, the responsibility of the business corporate is not limited to its owner, but it has assumed large dimensions—employees, consumers, suppliers, competitors, government, environment etc. and this responsibility of the business corporate, which includes the satisfaction of these parties along with the owner is called social responsibility of the business. In shaping India's future, the integration of the corporate sector into community development for all sections—class, caste, sex etc. with full social responsibility is a need of the hour; and the emotional, managerial and structural expertise of industry will help to build a stronger community at the micro-level in remote rural and local areas and at the macro-level of nation-building.

Notes

1. Sen, Samita, 2003, Women's Strikes, Gender and Class in the Bengal Jute Industry: 1890-1940, in Chanda, Anuradha; Sarkar, Mahua; Chattopadhyay, Kunal (eds.), *Women in History*, Kolkata: Progressive Publishers, p. 65.
2. Ray, Asok Kumar, (2008) Institutional Reforms, Governance and Growth: A Case Study of North-East India, in Ray, Asok Kumar, Satyabrata Chakraborty (eds.), *Society, Politics and Development in North-East India*, New Delhi: Concept Publishing Company Pvt. Ltd., p. 166.
3. Bhattacharjee, R.P., (2008), Impact of New Economic Policy in North-Eastern Region, in Dev, B.J.; Sengupta; Kiya, Ray; B. Dutta (eds.), *Globalization and North East India*, New Delhi, Concept Publishing Company Pvt. Ltd., p. 239.
4. Alic Sindzingre, (2008) Revisiting the links between Trade Openness, Poverty, Inequality and Growth: The Examples of India, in Preeti Phuskele (eds.), *Globalization—Impact and Implication*, ICFAI Books, pp. 207-08.
5. Giri, Pabitra, (2008) Implication of New Economic Policy for Development of North-East India, in Dev; B.J.; Sengupta, Kiya; Ray, B. Dutta (eds.), *Globalization and North-East India*, New Delhi: Concept Publishing Company Pvt. Ltd., p. 47.
6. Gautam, Deepika, Corporate Social Responsibility—Issues and Challenges, in Bansal, S.P.; Chandel, Kulbhushan and Singh, Raj Kumar (eds.), *Corporate Social Responsibility—Sustainable and Inclusive Growth*, New Delhi: Bharti Publication, p. 7.
7. Khurshed Alam, (2008) New Economic Policy and Assam's Economic Performance, in Dev, B.J.; Sengupta, Kiya; Ray, B. Dutta (eds.), *Globalization and North-East India*, New Delhi: Concept Publishing Company Pvt. Ltd., p. 71.
8. *Ibid.*
9. Gautam, Deepika, *op. cit.*, p. 4.
10. Patil, V.P., and Lokapur, I.A., (1983) Gandhian Concept of Trusteeship, in Patil, V.T. (Ed.) *Studies on Gandhi*, New Delhi: Sterling Publishers Pvt. Ltd., p. 99.
11. Sorokhaibam, Robita, (2006) An Overview of Women Entrepreneurship in Manipur, in Prasain, G.P. (ed.) *Entrepreneurship and Small Scale Industries*, New Delhi: Akanksha Publishing House, pp. 248-49.

12. *Interview* with M. Ranjana Devi, Elangbam Leikai, Imphal, Dt. 10-10-2013.
13. *Interview* with Smt. Yumnam Sarojini Devi, Yumnam Leikai, Imphal, Dt. 15-10-2013.
14. T. Davis, Understanding Entrepreneurship, in Emitio Congragado (ed.), *Measuring Entrepreneurship, Building a Statistical System.* Springer, University of Huelva, Spain.
15. A. Henia, (2008) Education and Women Empowerment, in Gassah, L.S. (ed.), *Women Empowerment Movement in North-East India,* New Delhi: Omson Publication, p. 81.
16. Sen, Samita, *op. cit.*, p. 74.
17. *Times of India*, p. 9, dt. 5.11.2013.
18. Batra, G.S., (2000), Some Aspects of Social Accounting in Corporate Sector Enterprises in India, in Batra, G.S. and Dangwal, R.C. (eds.) *Commerce and Business Research, New Horizon,* New Delhi: Deep and Deep Publication Pvt. Ltd., p. 72.

9
Extremism, Human Rights and Women

The post-colonial Indian States are built on contradictory principles of sovereign nation states, political obligations of the citizens and institutionalized force. In relation to North-East India the continual exposition of the institutionalized force on the part of the State has raised the fundamental question on the irreconcilable needs of territorial integrity and national security on the one hand and the need of adhering to the basic canons of human rights on the other. Consequently, a situation in which the imperatives of rule of law and the inevitability of the reign of terror challenged each other has been occurred. Whereas such extremism in the North-Eastern Region generally and especially in Manipur, posed a crisis to the ruling elites, both the rhetoric of mainstream and systemic integration—needed for consolidation of the nation-state were also challenged. On the other hand the issues of human rights arose out of the emerging trend. The State forces under such circumstances built its repressive image and such repression targeted not only to the extremists, but the civil populace too, who also struggle for a just and equitable social existence. Human rights and democracy are integrally linked to realizing substantive peace and security. It can be argued that the international discourse of human security approximates this multi-dimensional vision of peace. If the traditional security or national security has to do with protecting the State against aggression or internal disturbances, the catch all phrase 'human security' places the individual and the community as the subject and the measure of security discourses. As a corollary, the individuals and social groups define and identify security threats and are empowered to develop strategies for their own protection. Its natural consequence is the expectation that civil society groups will play a key role in security and conflict resolution.

Conditions for the Growth of Extrimism

In India, the State and society need to find ways of forging national unity amid the socio-cultural diversity. The world, ever more independent economically, cannot function unless people respect diversity and built unity through common bonds of humanity. The North-East Indian people are basically Mongoloid by race and remaining are mainly the Aryans. And like their distant predecessors and contemporary racial brethren, tribal tradition has been an intricate part of their lives since time immemorial. Western civilization has a general tendency to view the North-East India people as primitive and semi-human beings. To the rest of Indians, tribal people are uncivilized and backward people. Most of the writers who wrote about the people of the region branded North-East Indian people as backward people, while most anthropologists have a common view about North-East India that the people came from a very distinctive race since time immemorial. Whatever may be the name, the label backwardness can be turned into an asset.[1] Again, post-independent political system of North-East India generally and Manipur in particular is regularly threatened by destabilization. People felt no sign of economic satisfaction. North-East India, which occupies 9 per cent of the total geographical area of the country, i.e. 2,55,037 is a rural agro-based society and every woman participates in the agricultural programme. It has been over the years the practice of the people towards producing only sufficiently for each family. But, today in the name of modernization the traditional system has been ignored and even negatively affected to a certain degree. Modernization has to do with modern technology which is known to a few professional people, and the common people get displaced. Agriculture is the main occupation of the people of North-East India, but the region witnesses a highly deficit in food production. The land relation is chaotic although since 1951 many well meaning land reform measures have been enacted, they have not been implemented with seriousness. The region has fallen behind the rest of the country in terms of every yardstick of development in the field of oil, natural gas, eco-tourism, tea, herbal medicines etc. which are the unrecognized potentials of this region. The economic policies contributed to regional disparities too and declined in the working population. The New Economic Policy adopted by the Government of India in 1991 had the objective of integrating the Indian economy with the global economy. But till now, the New Economic Policy has marginal impact on the people of North-East India. This is due to economic backwardness of the region with the semi-feudal anarchy in land relations which is the basic anchor of the economy of the region. But in urban areas, new wants and new aspirations among the neo-middle class are being created. Gradually, the people of North-East India came to realize the importance of their existence, and along with the fast changing world, they woke up for self-determination. Today almost the entire North-East India is in flames with the desire for self-determination. Perhaps, nowhere in the country except North-East India is there such a peculiar situation, resulting in so much confusion and disturbance? Human dignity is very often denied. Human rights are violated much. Most of the States are politically restricted and one after another black laws are imposed.[2] Today, the indigenous people are not secure in the hands of the more advanced people. Seventy five million indigenous people scattered throughout the country have come to this realization of their existence in the last few years: the Jharkhand, Uttarakhand, Bilkham, Chhattisgarh, Vidarbha, Gorkhaland, and all seven States of North-East India. Their struggle is political, social, cultural and economic—in fact multy-pronged. The process of struggle may differ and may be called extremism, militancy, terrorism, or whatever; but they are all fighting for a cause.[3] This is happened mainly as a result of the shifting of values and ownership. Today, the country is surviving with the natural resources of the indigenous people's land. Fifty per cent of the mineral resources, most of the beautiful national parks, and almost all the virgin forest in the country belong to the indigenous people. And yet, the poorest people in the country are the indigenous people. They have become miserable because they are exploited left and right by the so-called civilized and rich people and conditionally poor indigenous people displaced from their own soil. Rich people become the owner of the poor indigenous people. In one term, the indigenous people have no financial power for becoming the owners of the new economic opportunities provided by the liberalized economic system. Before they could understand this sudden changing process, they found themselves already discriminated as universalized and outcast in their own land. Few elite and educated people of the region are also fusion with the new culture. The educated and professional citizens are supposed to be collective sources of generating power to society. They do not take the initiative to provide a better life. They become selfish and withdraw themselves to their comfortable lives. To them village life is of old fashion. Their ancestral place and kinsmen in the village are only pieces for museums. To them society means little. They have no shame although their villages are backward. They have no mind to improve the living conditions of those settled in the villages owing to various reasons. Their education is not relevant to their society. Dr. M.M. Thomas rightly remarked that high techno-culture has produced the technocrat and the bureaucrat and the power of the State is, so that, the structure of democratic participation of the people has been weakened.[4] Natural resources were plundered to make profit for newcomers, lands were alienated from tribal, and even their original tribal names changed and defined in non-tribal terms. The climate of the lands inhabited by the tribal have greatly changed and this has adversely affected the flora and fauna, and agricultural use as well. Modern machine and machine made products tried to spread in every nook and corner of the country. An active consumer culture is coming up in urban societies. As a result, the traditional skills of women of North-East India in the fields of agriculture and new technology penetrated in the traditional fields and small scale industries. New land owning classes are emerging. The small men and women are pushed to the margin.[5] Immigration does play a role in the conflicts more as a cause of the alienation of land, water and biodiversity around which they have built their culture, economy and identity than as an ethnic issue. Given close link between land, culture and identity, they view the shortages the immigrants cause as attacks on their identity. They react at first to the dominant groups from outside the region whom they consider responsible for the shortages and have failed to make productive investment. Thus, central to the debate on immigration is land and lack of investment. Slowly, this conflict shifts to the ethnic communities of the region when they perceive as competitors for scarce resources. The problem of unemployment in the North-East India has been increasing in its intensity.

The North-East region of India is known for its social and economic backwardness as well as never ending story of social and political instability and poor political delivery system. There is a great need for a participatory human development, the investment in human beings themselves by means of

Table 9.1: No. of Technical and Non-technical Institutions in some States of India

Universities		*Engineering Institutions*	
States	*Number*	*States*	*Number*
Bihar	15	Bihar, Gujarat	37
Delhi	17	Punjab	45
Gujarat	17	West Bengal	54
Rajasthan	20	Madhya Pradesh	61
West Bengal	20	Uttar Pradesh	89
Karnataka	23	Karnataka	118
Uttar Pradesh	34	Maharashtra	155
Tamil Nadu	35	Andhra Pradesh	236
Maharashtra	42	Tamil Nadu	254
North-eastern States (Seven States)	**15**	North-eastern States (Seven States)	**10**

Source: *The Times of India*, dt. 6.11. 2006, p. 3.

education and training, i.e. human capital is quite necessary. Again in the pattern of human capital accumulation, youth constitutes the latent resource of human resource development.

There is a symbol of biasness in connection with the opening of higher and technical educational institutions when it is compared between the North-eastern States and other States of India. Table 9.1 shows the exact number of technical and non-technical educational institutions in different States of India which can depict the exact figure of variation.

At the stage of youth we can impart, train, nurture skills and help them to maintain good health. Unfortunately, substantial section of the youth does not get the opportunity to go for training or better higher education. Even those who do get the training and education do not get proper or even minimum employment. Today the trend of unemployed youth signals a major crisis in the human resource development. The crisis sometimes responds negative human capital investment.[6] The number of unemployed youth registered in the employment exchange crossed over six lakh in March 2009 in Manipur. The negative responses arising as a result directly make erosion in the human capital. Such erosion in the human capital is caused by drug abuse, addiction of alcohol, tobacco and infection through HIV virus in the name of unemployment, lack of capital and infrastructure and frustration. Lack of employment opportunities contributed to the growth of hopelessness and frustration among the youth of the region leading to militancy in them. They feel alienated from the rest of the country, particularly those who live in the periphery and having trans-boarder kinship. Some groups no doubt speak in terms of right to self-determination, meaning thereby right to secession from the country. Some of the militant groups speak vaguely of socialist preference of the new order they dream of and some of them do not indicate any idealistic commitment.[7]

The terms terrorism, insurgency, civil war, guerrilla warfare, intimidation and extremism are most often interchangeable terms and are used very loosely. This is because of the fact that 'violence' is common in all the terms.

But the two terms 'terrorism' and 'insurgency' have different meanings. An insurgent is a national of a country who is in revolt against the government of his/her country and fights to overthrow the government by the guerrilla warfare. While the terrorist may or may not be a national of the country in which he operates. Insurgency has its roots both in the socio-economic and political environment of the region/State and also in the strong local urge to safeguard the identity. It can be encountered not by military force or by any coercive Act, but by gradual effort to understand its root cause and to understand the effects on the civil society. Insurgency or extremism is an internal problem, but the results of these problems are more serious than the external one. We argue that it is the internal socio-economic, political, cultural and identity issues that sustained by the insurgencies are more than the external one. This section, will, therefore, take up primarily the issues of human insecurity and try to argue that human insecurity is primarily responsible for the continuing recruitment of the insurgents. Unemployment, poverty, a feeling of relative deprivation, corruption, underdevelopment, and devastation caused natural calamities are among the factors that act as a breeding ground for insurgency. The economy failed to meet the growing aspirations of the people particularly the younger generation. This in turn, provides a fertile ground for the militant groups to groom them for their outfits.

Different scholars are giving different opinions regarding the causes for extremism and insurgency, but one of the main causes in Manipur is growing unemployment of the educated youth and the economic backwardness of the region especially after the merger of Manipur to the Indian Union. Psychologists observed that when certain situations come into direct confrontations with the established norms of behaviour, it creates alienation and discontent. This alienation grows from economic, political, cultural and ethnological inequalities. It makes individuals feel worthless, meaningless and estranged. The socio-political environment of India and her attitude towards the people of North-East India and towards particular ethnic groups thereof is one of the main causes of alienation and insecurity in the minds and hearts of the people of the region.[8] These tendencies reflect perceived inadequacies of sub-regional political systems that lead to the emergence of different over-ground and underground movements in the region. The origin of such type of movements is not recent. Contemporary movements of any society, not only in this region, in the sphere of economy, politics or culture are inspired by conscious national motives and urges, irrespective of whether they are organized to defend and develop the freedom and culture of respective notions or to mitigate or suppressed the freedom or culture of other nations. The irreconcilability over the years has incubated the process of extremism by the groups in this region, often challenging the over-arch of the sovereign States of India. Theoretically, the nature of extremism is political, but practically, acts of violence are the main methodology subscribed to, and targeted socio-political and economic changes of the whole society. During the British Imperialism, the militant nationalist or the extremist drew inspiration from the India's past, invoked the great episodes in the history of the Indian people, and tried to infuse national pride and self-respect among them. The militant nationalists were distinguished for the great qualities of immense self-sacrifice and suffering for the cause of freedom. They constituted the first batch of martyrs in the nationalist movement. Their very programme brought them into conflict with the Government. They experienced imprisonment and deportations and suffered privations.[9] Today, extremism has most commonly become identified with individuals or groups attempting to overthrow existing political institutions, often substituting violent acts like kidnapping, assassinations, bombings and hijackings for legitimate political activities. Extremism has become the detested thing for the civilized nation. The statecraft of colonial interventions and the whole idea of mainstreaming frontier space have created resentment among native communities. Similarly, ethnic identities, constructions of the 'others' is gaining new meaning as autonomy movements have succeeded in instigating federal state in the region. Ethnicity feels like a double edged sword. It unites most communities for political demands from outsiders but fails to organize the communities within as a common entity. These observations show that ethnic tension and conflicts have been a part of the North-Eastern reality. After a look at the ethnic differences within each State, a reflection will follow on the immigrant issue. We will look at the implications of this stand and see whether that is the only alternative.[10] Insurgency in this context has to be understood as a contest over nationalism and a struggle to sustain the plurality of social forms and community life. The ethno-political and ethno-nationalistic demands contests as well as rearticulate the web of political culture that has been formalized by colonial forms of governance, based on power, privilege, and patronage in the highlands and foothills of North-East India. One finds a large variety of conflict dynamics in this region ranging from sovereignty and autonomy to terrorism and ethnic clashes. No other region of India, South Asia or the world must have seen the existence of so numerous ethnic based insurgent outfits as North-East India does, nor does any known part of the world witness the proliferation and mushrooming of militant outfits as in this region. Thus, it forms a complex matrix. It has been facing the onslaught of ethnicity-based armed conflicts since the late 1940s. Violent and vociferous demands by various ethnic groups for sovereignty or for new states have been occurring over the past five decades. To it one may add the problem of continuous inflow of migrants and the fight over resources.[11]

The people of Manipur as represented by the armed nationalists groups or extremists strongly questioned the legal validity and democratic basis of Manipur integration with India. It now becomes obvious that there has not been any legality and constitutional validity as per the provisions of International Laws and the Manipur State Constitution Act, 1947. Besides, all the provisions of the agreements were in the nature of personal agreements between the Dominion of India and the Maharaja as a person and not as a head of State. It also does not give any reference to any State machinery as Manipur had a responsible Government before the ȧgreement for the nature of relation.

Manipur was an independent princely State for about two thousand years. Unfortunately, Manipur lost her independence in the Anglo-Manipuri war of 1891 and became a part (though not annexed) of the British Empire. But with the passing of the Indian Independence Act, 1947, Manipur once again remained her sovereign status. It for the first time in its history adopted a democratically elected Legislative Assembly with the Maharaja as a titular head of the State. The society in Manipur during the period 1947 to 1949 remained stable. The social order was mainly based on Hinduism. The section of the educated class got enlarged. Most of them got employment in Government jobs enjoying higher status in the society.[12] The Standstill Agreement did not infringe upon the sovereignty of Manipur as nothing in either of those agreements include the exercise of anyway of acceptance of any future Constitution of India. Therefore, the Standstill Agreement and the Instrument of Accession did not affect the sovereignty of Manipur and the same were superseded by the Indian Independence Act of 1947. When India got Independence in 1947, the suzerainty of the British Crown and the rulers of the Indian States were also finished. Consequently, Manipur also became an Independent State on 14th August, 1947, legally and technically free from the British Parliament and the British India. As for Dominion Agent or the Dewan, it was an extra-constitutional body, which was extra-judiciously appointed. Therefore, the Dominion Agent or the Dewan could not affect the sovereignty of Manipur. But the nature of the functioning of the political authority exercised by the Chief Commissioner had given a negative impact on the peaceful and stable social order of Manipur. The concentration of the political power in the hands of the Chief Commissioner who acted on behalf of the President of India had created dissatisfaction in the minds of the people of Manipur. The members of the Advisery Council, as the name indicates, were only advisers to the Chief Commissioner. The later was not bound to accept the advice given by the advisers. The people of Manipur had started movements demanding higher political status of Manipur.[13] But the response of the Government of India was slow and minimum which they have learnt from the British colonizers. And again the repressive measures were so serious even the Britishers did not employ.

The Government of India employs Armed Forces Special Power Act (AFSPA), POTA, TADA and many other draconian laws as devices to institutionalize violence against the people with an aim to build legitimacy of the State activities. It is worth stating that the desperate resort to naked use of force only indicates the erosion of legitimacy of the Government of India. As we know, force is necessary to extract obedience from the masses only when there exist a crisis of legitimacy. This infers that the open resistance of the people in the recent past against the Government demonstrated the degree of allegiance, which the people of Manipur owe towards the established system. The frequent resort to brute force underscores the very fact that Indian rule in Manipur is sustained through perpetration of violence against the natives in the absence of popular base among the masses. This exposes the truth that Indian rule in Manipur lacks consent, legitimacy and mandate, which constitute the core issue of the nationalist movements in Manipur.

Post-colonial North-East India as a political, geographical and cultural entity present these contests over identities as pure acts of 'develop mentalities' thus negating the cultural and historical context in which these communities were organized and imagined towards the idea of India. The struggle for sovereignty has very quickly turned into armed struggle which the Indian State has officially designated as insurgencies. Naturally, the tension and violence generated, initially by the Governments violent response towards the extra-constitutional strategy adopted by the various political groups located in different States of the region quickened the process of conflicts. The Indian states resort to such armed struggle was also an armed solution both in the shape of considerable army operations and police action of various degrees of intensity.

Thus, the continuing attacks and counter-attacks lead to further alienation and exclusion of the region.[14]

The security issue is one more point of tension between the indigenous people and the State in South Asia. Its main reason is that until recently by 'sovereignty' one meant Independence, and self-determination was understood as the right to secede.[15] Many nuances have been introduced in this thinking in the last two decades. After a two decades long struggle the Mizo leaders accepted being a State within the Indian Union, but with their civil affairs run under Art. 371G. The NSCN-IM has been speaking of a State with its own Constitution that begins with a reference to the Constitution of India. The nature of this reference is yet to be defined, but a beginning has been made towards autonomy within the Indian Union. It is called sovereignty and its understanding is involving slowly, but it is clear that many in the NSCN-IM have moved away from the Phizo doctrine.

Peace Processes

The history of resolving conflicts in India shows that the State is after a piecemeal approach. The response of the Indian State to some of the intractable ethnic insurgencies in the North-East has so far been to divide the rebel organizations and attempt to control them with the help of the renegades, corrupt the leaders of insurgent groups in front of the public by providing them a luxurious lifestyle when they come out for talks 'buy time' as much as possible in the name of negotiation, physically eliminate the family members of persons belonging to the rebel organizations, develop and help counter-insurgency forces, use maximum State power with the help of the police and the army appoint retired army generals, police and intelligence chiefs as Governors in the insurgency affected regions and put all the draconian laws into practice.[16] After a considerable period of time when the armed groups get tired and the people are fed up, the State imposes an accord, the provisions of which are rarely implemented. It is not that such accords resolve ethnic issues. They only give provisional respite to the State and provide a face saving exit to the leaders of the militant organizations who immediately capture power of their respective states and become a part of the State machinery. In such gambling of power, which is played in the name of the people, the real issues are always sidelined until they are taken by a new brand of leadership.

The conflict resolution process conducted in North-East India is at an elite level so far and is generally aimed at political concessions without involving representatives of the civil society. If the terms of peace are imposed on the people, this may perpetuate traditional power structures rather than bring about social change. In general, it is important that civil society representatives and non-combatant groups have some say in the design and implementation of the peacemaking and peace-building agenda because they are the real sufferer of the conflict situations as well as they might have certain clear knowledge about issues of violence developed in the area concerned. This does not mean that all parties must be directly involved in the negotiations. This requires those persons who can represent and communicate both the parties. The Assam movement (1979-1985) is a clear example of how an accord can create mistrust, fissures and multiplications of identities among various ethnic groups. The Assam accord was understood to be the Constitutional protection mechanism for the Asamiya speaking people. This has led to the others struggling for their own protection mechanism. Great then was their disenchantment with the Assam accord which sought to protect Assamese identity and culture, but made no mention of tribal identities. Moreover, most of the provisions are yet to be implemented.[17] The situation became deteriorated in Assam day after day. So, without any invitation, Mamoni Goswami requested the Central Government to control troops engaged in counter-insurgency operation against the outlawed ULFA in view of the current peace initiatives and to create a congenial atmosphere to bring the rebels to the negotiation table. With a motherly feeling, Dr. Mamoni Goswami spoke in the peace process and also stressed the need for extensive study of the problems that would help formulation of a holistic plan for amicable settlement of insurgency. With a relentless effort and conscious, the ULFA also agreed to send a nine members people's consultative group to initiate the discussion with the Central Government. Even though the issue is not, still, at a final stage, her effort could be regarded as the most important step towards attaining peace in the State.

The Indian States resort to repressive measures in the name of protecting national sovereignty and territorial integrity. Thus, the atrocities committed by the Governmental forces towards the people of Manipur secured legitimacy through State sponsored legislations. The conflict situation prevailing in Manipur is not a law and order issue as depicted by the Indian propaganda machineries. It remains conspicuous that the resistance movement spearheaded by the dissenting nationalist groups has gained a great momentum despite stringent military operation launched by the Indian Armies and Paramilitary forces under the immunity granted by the Government of India and its legislations. The State and non-State armed groups think of peace only as absence of armed conflict, but most people of the region perceived it as a new society based on justice. Such a new society cannot be achieved without understanding the causes of conflicts and attempting a solution to them. There is a perception gap between Government and the people of the region which should be bridged without delay by constant interaction between the two. North-East India has become a victim of easy money poured by the Central Government which has affected the ethics and social structure of the people instead of assured sustained development. Most of the peace-building exercises conducted in North-East India are in the form of reconstructive peace building. These exercises attempt to address the political aspects which are by and large associated with the capturing of political power and end up in accord centric politics. The assumption in this exercise is that once sovereignty is attained and a homeland is granted, all the issues affecting the people will be taken care of. Issues arising from the conflict situation such as the plight of women, children, the IDPS etc. are conveniently forgotten both by the State and non-State actors.

The growing gap between the communities in conflict cannot be brushed aside as the diabolic tactic of the State. Perhaps, here lies an effective role of the civil society and the sustained effort of the civil society organizations for a democratic resolution of conflicts through dialogue and negotiations.

In Manipur, violation of Human Rights coupled with gendered violence. Gender-based violence encompasses a wide range of human rights violation, including sexual abuse of children, rape, domestic violence, sexual assault and harassment, trafficking of women and girls and several harmful traditional practices. Anyone of these abuses can leave deep psychological scars, damage the health of women and girls in general, including their reproductive and sexual health, and in some instances, result in death. Violence against women has been recognized as "the most pervasive yet least recognized human rights abuse in the world." Accordingly, the Vienna Human Rights Conference and the Fourth World Conference on Women gave priority to this issue which jeopardizes women's lives, bodies, psychological integrity and freedom. Violence against women and girls constitute the single most prevalent and universal violation of human rights. The United Nations, in keeping with the spirit of the UN Declaration of Human Rights, work in many ways to eliminate this morally unacceptable scourge. UN Conference on Human Rights, the 1979 Convention on the Elimination of All forms of Discrimination Against Women (CEDAW), the Beijing Declaration, the United Nations Development Fund for Women (UNDFW) etc. are some of the instruments that would address the issue of gendered violence. Despite regard for the principle of non-discrimination in the enjoyment of rights contained in the UDHR, ICCPR, ICESCR, and other human rights instruments, women were not treated equally at the global level.[18] CEDAW acknowledged that discrimination against women violates the principles of equality of rights and respect for human dignity, and is an obstacle to the participation of women, on equal terms with men, in the political, social, economic and cultural life of their countries. This in turn, affects the development of family and society as a whole. In the armed conflict situation in Manipur many people are killed and kidnapped, including the innocent one. Many newly married and unmarried women are forced to commit suicide to save themselves against rape and social abuse by the security forces. With the increase of state violence in the state particularly against the youth and women, the women community in Manipur staged unrobed protest march against custodial rape and killing of Ms Manorama by the Assam Rifles personnel on 11th July, 2004.

Really the accords signed with the initiation of the Government are failed to address the nature of 'discord'. The people's confidence in these peace accords is decreasing now a days. One of the basic reasons of it is the failure of the Central Government to implement the terms of agreement arrived at such 'accord'. The accords made by the Central Government are locked up in a box, and key is thrown into the deep sea. Had it not been the case, there would not have been serious problems in Nagaland after Shillong Accord of 1975. In such conditions, the common people of any community are being victimized both by the insurgency and the Government. In the battle of power between these two groups, the innocent people need to take initiatives to free themselves from the dangers from both the State and non-State actors.

Issues of Human Rights

Human rights violation accounting in the State of Manipur during the last thirty to forty years has gone to the extreme. After merging to the Indian Union, Manipur has witnessed the emergence of various dissenting nationalist groups launching a systematic and sustained military campaign against the Government of India to defend their sovereign nationhood. But, the responses of the Government of India to such indigenous reactions came in terms of enacting numerous black laws and deployment of armed forces resulting into militarization of Manipur. It was only in the late 1960s that the demand for self-determination came to be debated and discussed in the political circle. Before 1970s and 1980s numerous underground groups emerged which have been designated as insurgent by the Indian state.[19] The logical consequence of such a conflict-situation is the violation of human rights and civil liberties on a wide scale. Now-a-days, the notion of national security, law and order, national integration etc. have become powerful justificatory doctrines of state violence against the civil population.

During this period there have been innumerable told and untold incidents of violation of human rights. The violations included arrest, detention, disappearances, custodial tortured and killing, atrocities, rape and sexual violence to women and so on by the armed forces in the name of controlling the extremism committed by the armed nationalists groups in State. The other dimension of human rights violation arises from the factional fights among the underground organizations that often take the toll of human rights. Manipur also witnessed the violations of human rights among members of the different underground organizations. Though working and struggling together for the common cause and common ideology, the members of the underground organizations killed each other whenever any disagreement or factional interest developed within the organization.[20] Distrust and disagreement within the factional forces within the underground organizations like NSCN (IM) and NSCN (K), and the different Kuki underground organizations in Manipur. Besides violation of human rights by the militant organizations themselves is not to loose sight of, ambushing the army in the public place, encounter between the State and non-State actors, cross fire, planting explosives and many other acts of this nature ended valuable lives of many civilians. Apart from huge human cost arising of the insurgency and counter-insurgency in the State, the magnitude of social cost in terms of fear psychosis, melancholy, financial extortion became serious human rights concerns. On 1st September, 2007, the then Union Home Minister Sivraj Patil gave the Status Report in connection with the violence and terror in North-East India. According to his statement, the rate of violence is highest in Assam among the North-East States that is followed by Manipur, Nagaland and

Tripura.[21] In terms of the number of victims, his statement is quite right. But after a clear analysis with reference to the total number of population and the rate of percentage of violence up to June 30, 2007, Manipur is higher than Assam according to the Status Report (Table 9.2).

Table 9.2: Terror Attack and Killings in North-East India

Name of States	*Total no. of population*	*Killed*			
		Civilian	*Security personel*	*Total*	*Per cent*
Assam	26655528	156	15	171	0.00064
Manipur	2293896	72	25	97	0.0004229

The draconian acts including AFSPA are imposing in the State and violated every canon of democracy and human rights. Growing militarization of the society made civil life miserable. Instead of aiding the civil power as stipulated in the act, the armed forces made the civilians equal targets of State violence in the name of containing underground organizations.

Extra Judicial Killings by Security Forces

Children and Civilian Victims

1. Th. Netaji of Kakwa, February 28, 1996.
2. Kangjam Ojit, Iroisemba: September 25, 1997.
3. Y. Iboyaima *alias* Ukabi of Awang Potsangbam: March 19, 2002.
4. Th. Dhirendra of Naorem Leikai: April 6, 2002.
5. Md. Jane Alam of Hatta: August 1, 2002.
6. Thangtinsein Kipgen and Limbertlen: August 2008.

(*Source*: Media information collected by the author.)

The wholesale counter terrorism of the power, state perpetually threatened the basic principle of civic republicanism, shutters right to movement of the citizens, and right to life and liberty of them. The counter-insurgency is indiscriminate, and affects the civic zones badly. On the other hand the militant terrorists in order to disseminate terrorism implicate the entire civil society and tend to universalize terrorism through their acts in public places. This causes casualties not only to the State forces, but also to the civil populace. Thus, the powers, state and the insurgents had pressed the civil society and reduce civic rights.

List of Some Major Incidents of Gross Human Rights Violations in Manipur:

1. Heirangoithong Massacre: March 14, 1984.
2. Operation Blue Bird at Oinam: July 10, 1987.
3. Tera Bazar Massacre: March 25, 1993.
4. RIMC Massacre, January 7, 1995.
5. Tonsem Lamkhai Killing: October 4, 1998.
6. Malom Massacre: November 2, 2000.
7. The Great June Uprising: June 18th, 2001.
8. Leplen Mass Torture: 2002.
9. Pangei Bazar Firing: April 9, 2002.
10. Sharajeevan Bomb Blast, Paona Bazar: October, 2007.
11. Ragailong Bomb Blast: October 2008.

(*Source*: Media information collected by the author.)

The social and psychological cost of insurgency and counter-insurgency cannot be measured through quantitative terms, increasing anxiety, unpredictability of life, liberty and fragile peace feature of the State. There are innumerable cases of disappearance of the youth and involuntary migration of the youth community from the State.

Reinforce Disappearances and Killings

1. Loken and Lokendro of Basikhong: September 23, 1980.
2. C. Poul and C. Daniel of Ukhrul: March 10, 1982.
3. L. Bijoikumar of Thangmeiband: June 5-6, 1996.
4. Mr. Mahaimi of Ukhrul: 1995.
5. Y. Sanamacha of Angtha: February 12-13, 1998.
6. Boyai of Kwakeithel: 1998.
7. Md. Tayeb Ali of Kairang: July 25, 1995.

8. Baby Luiningla: November 2003.
9. W. Rishikanta: November 2008.

(*Source*: Media information collected by the author.)

In Manipur, Sharmila Chanu has been fasting since, 2000 November in protest against the violent actions committed by the armed personnel in the name of the maintenance of law and order in the State, and mainly, she is demanding the repeal of Armed Forces Special Power Act, 1958—in the name of this Act a lot of innocent people have lost their lives in the hands of the armed personnel. She faced the cases of committing suicide, but her statement clarified that she has been fasting as a movement only for repealing Armed Forces Special Power Act. Her lawyer, Khaidem Mani Singh analyze, whole details of the condition so, the judgement was given that there is no proof that Sharmila has any intention for committing suicide so, she was released from the jail on 20th August, 2014, but rearrested again on 22nd August, 2014. Noted human right activist Babloo Loitongbam said, "India has been the focus on the human rights discourse in recent times. This is an unprecedented opportunity for the country to re-examines its human rights performance with reference to women's rights."

Issues of Women

In the conflict prone areas of the country, the issues of women are vulnerable. They are both direct and indirect victims of the conflict situations. However, when we look into depth, women's contribution in the process of peace is uncountable—the society may recognize or not recognized it does not matter to them. The feminist perspective of violence highlights the negative impact of war on women. It states that the female body is subject to assault and abuse during the course of conflict. Instruments of dominance like rape are employed on the women of the opposition party. Defiling women is seen also as defiling of the whole people of the community. Gender-based violence encompasses a wide range of human rights violations including sexual abuse of children, rape, domestic violence, sexual assault and harassment, trafficking of women and girls and several harmful traditional practices. Anyone of these abuses can leave deep psychological scars, damage of health of women and girls in general including their reproductive and sexual health, and in some instances, results in death.

Rape Cases Committed by Security Personnel and Killing

1. Miss Rose of Ukhrul: March 4, 1974.
2. Mrs. Ahanjaobi: 1996.
3. Mrs. Pramo of Moirang: 1998.
4. Mrs. Mercy of Lamdan: 2000.
5. Mrs. Bina of Luwangsangbam Matai Village: 2001.
6. Miss N. Sanjita of Jiribam: October 5, 2003.
7. Laisram Bimola Devi and Laisram Manisang Devi, Pukhao Ahalup Awang Leikai: 1999.
8. Ch. Jamini Devi, Yairipok: 1999.
9. Thangjam Manorama Devi: 2004.

(*Source*: Media information collected by the author.)

Ethnic classes occur in North-East India in this post-colonial period by giving charges to the British policy or the failure of the governance in India after Independence. But the conflict induced displacement is a serious concern which has both long-term and short-term consequences for women. In such ethnic clashes, displacement affects women enormously and causes physical, mental and economic insecurity. It makes them more vulnerable to trafficking and sexual abuse. When the basic needs of women in relief camps are not met, the issues of their safety remain a distant agenda for the Government. A 2011 report by the Norwagian Internal Displacement Monitering Centre stated that about 4,50,000 people were displaced in the North-East in the year, with 1,70,000 displaced in Assam alone. In 2012, about 4 lakh people were displaced in the violence that broke out in BTAD. This is considered to be the highest in modern history.[22]

There is an urgent need for adopting a dynamic approach requiring a new orientation in policy perception remembering that the people are one. We need to create a climate in North-East India, so that, every citizen of the region feels assured that his or her language, culture and distinct identity are secured and will remain so in India for ever. For this, the crucial requirement is creation of conditions for meaningful community participation at every level through greater decentralization of power, political and economic, ensuring equitable distribution and sustainable use of productive resources and capability and skills of the people of the region. It suggested a better coordinated development strategy for North-East India and a strong and transparent political will to instill a sense of participation in the minds of the people of the hills and the valleys.

Notes

1. Nuh, V.K., 2001, *Struggle for Identity in North-East India,* Spectrum Publication, Guwahati, p. 88.
2. *Ibid.*, p. 14.
3. *Ibid.*, p. 20.
4. *Ibid.*, p. 99.
5. Ray, B. Dutta, Dev, Bimal J.; Sengupta, Kiya (eds.) 2008, *Globalization and North-East India,* Concept Publishing Company Pvt. Ltd., New Delhi, p. 4.
6. Th. Binarani Devi, 2008, India's Look East Policy and Youth of Manipur, in Ray, B. Dutta, Dev, Bimal J.; Sengupta, Kiya, (eds.) *Globalization and North-East India,* Concept Publishing Company Pvt. Ltd., New Delhi, pp. 320-21.
7. Pakem, B., 1997, *Insurgency in North-East India,* Omson Publications, New Delhi, p. V.
8. Th. Binarani Devi, 2007, Insurgency and Human Rights in Manipur, in B.J. Dev and Asok Kumar Ray (eds.) *Terrorism and Human Rights in North-East India,* Om Publications, New Delhi, p. 118.
9. Ksh. Bimola Devi, 2008, Society and Politics in Manipur, in Ray, Asok Kumar and Chakraborty, Satyabrata, (eds.) *Society, Politics and Development in North-East India,* Concept Publishing Company Pvt. Ltd., New Delhi, p. 103.
10. Zehol Lucy, 2008, Ethnic Tension and Conflict: North-Eastern Experience, in Fernandes, Walter (ed.), *Search for Peace with Justice,*

Issues Around Conflict in North-East India, North-Eastern Social Research Centre, Guwahati, p. 46.

11. Binalaxmi Nepram Mentschel, 2008, Armed Conflicts and Small Arms Proliferation in North-East India, in Fernandes, Walter (ed.), *Search for Peace with Justice, Issues Around Conflict in North-East India*, North-Eastern Social Research Centre, Guwahati, pp. 85-86.
12. Ksh. Bimola Devi, *op. cit.*, pp. 103-04.
13. Desai, A.R., 1986, *Social Background of Indian Nationalism*, Popular Prakashan, Bombay, p. 333.
14. Karna, M.N., 2008, Conflicts amid the historical experiences of Identity, Nation and the State in North-Eastern India, in Fernandes, Walter (ed.), *Search for Peace with Justice, Issues Around Conflict in North-East India*, North-Eastern Social Research Centre, Guwahati, p. 25.
15. Fernandes, Walter, Bharali, Gita; Kezo, Vemedo, 2007, *The UN Indegenous Decade in North-East India*, North-Eastern Social Research Centre, Guwahati, p. 143.
16. Mahanta, Nani Gopal, 2008, What Makes Assam—A Perpetual Conflict Zone? Going Beyond Management to Conflict Transformation, in Fernandes, Walter (ed.), *Search for Peace with Justice, Issues Around Conflict in North-East India*, North-Eastern Social Research Centre, Guwahati, pp. 109-10.
17. Human Rights Documentation Centre, Introducing Human Rights, South Asia, Oxford University Press, New Delhi, p. 155.
18. Mahanta, Nani Gopal, *op. cit.*, p. 115.
19. Karna, M.N., *op. cit.*, p. 24.
20. Ksh. Bimola Devi, 2007, Violation of Human Rights and Peace Initiative in Manipur, in B.J. Dev and Asok Kumar Ray (eds.) *Terrorism and Human Rights in North-East India*, Om Publications, New Delhi, pp. 112-13.
21. *Poknapham* (Manipuri Local Daily), Dt. 2/9/2007, p. 1.
22. *Times of India*, dt. 20.08.2014, p. 2.

Conclusion

Society is a term which designates the whole network of relationship—family, caste, school, sports, club, trade union, chamber of commerce, fine arts circle, and many other groups and associations are formed. It is much more than a mere group of individuals. In the modern world, we take it for granted that all men and women are members of society. People's dependence on society is complete, and he/she cannot imagine living well and comfortably as he does today without the help of society. From the cradle to the grave, every minute people needs it and have to be highly indebted to it. Human being has been able to achieve much in civilization and culture only as a member of society. Society does not remain silent; it is change from one form to another without any fix time interval. A massive social transformation or change had its inevitable effect on the sphere of political mobilization.

Different school of thoughts give different ideas regarding this. According to the socialist thinkers, man and society cannot be separated; both have equal importance in human development. Despite remaining an integral part of society, man still retains his individuality and so is different from society. Man develops his desires, aspirations and activities through interdependence and exchange. Here, man is not different from society, but where man develops his desires, aspirations and activities and established interdependence in society, he is also different. Man is limited by his feelings. One who experiences law, happiness, fear and grief, is a complete man. These feelings are not a common experience; they cannot be exchanged or substituted. Exchange is a bridge between man and society. The fundamental base of an individual is his emotions and that of society is exchange. Again, according to some sociologists, society is a matrix of life sustaining relationship. Emotions are neither established nor are they life-sustaining. They are intrinsic to man from the perspective of life-sustenance, society is reality. There is no conflict here. Man lives comfortably only with the assumption that is real and keeping this in mind, safeguards social norms and values. Studies on the rights of women and their problems should be taken from the individualistic and sociological point of view. The claim of the rights of women is as a part of the society. There are no conditions as stated by the individualistic thinkers that man can live without society, he (man) was an individual in his own rights; that for the security of his property, rights and life or for the attainment of some other goals, man created society.

Gender stereotyping and violence at the domestic and social levels are some of the ongoing manifestation. The main causes of gender inequality are related to social and economic structure, which is based on informal and formal norms and practices. Consequently, the access of women, particularly those belonging to weaker sections including Scheduled Castes/ Scheduled Tribes/Other Backward Classes and minorities, majority of whom are in the rural areas and in the informal, unorganized sector to education, health and productive resources, among others, is inadequate. There they remain largely marginalized, poor and socially excluded. Barbaric and savagist practices still continue to haunt women in the form of female foeticide, child labour, child marriage, dowry, rape, sexual harassment, gender inequality, molestation, eve teasing, forced prostitution, child pornography etc. The increasing number of early widowhood is in an alarming stage in this armed conflict region, as well as the area of golden triangle where the number of HIV/AIDS is in a remarkable stage. In our contemporary industrial society women are much deprived, defected and dominated by men.

In the traditional conservative and sexually repressed Indian social context, women are seen as a target to be taken advantage of it. Women as a weaker section of the respective societies are suffering from different type of violence. Still they are struggling for the issues of violence in different parts of the globe, as for example that is happening in the State of Manipur. In all the movements against the violation of human rights in this insurgency and counter-insurgency prone area of Manipur, women are coming at the forefront. They organized different movements, giving pressure to the Government, and non-governmental organizations too, for bringing a just society where all can enjoy their full potentials. Their way of movement is something different from other movements in certain occasions. Women's role and activities in such movements are not only in the interest of women, but for the sake of the whole society. And peaceful democratic movements are ruthlessly suppressed; people's just demands are not entertained and simply gunned down. Communal violence, extra judicial killings, rape, molestation and torture and killing of women by the State and non-State actors, even by their near and dear ones, custodial torture, extortion etc. had crossed over the passed records. In the name of the maintenance of law and order in some part of the country, the government imposed Acts, but that violates the basic minimum rights of the people. The Armed Forces Special Power Act, 1958, is a case in point. Keeping in view the duty of the Union under Art. 355 of the Constitution, *inter alia* to protect every State against internal disturbance, it is considered desirable that the Central Government should also have power to declare areas as 'disturbed', to enable its armed forces to exercise the special powers. Section 3 of the AFSPA reads as follows—"power to declare areas to be disturbed areas—If, in relation to any State or Union Territory to which this Act extends, the Governor of that State or the Administrator of that Union Territory or the Central Government, in either case, is of the opinion that the whole or any part of such State or Union Territory, as the case may be, in such a disturbed or dangerous condition that the use of armed forces in aid of the civil power is necessary, the Governor of that State or the Administrator of that Union Territory or the Central Government, as the case may be, may, by notification in the Official Gazette, declare the whole or such part of such State or Union Territory to be a disturbed area." Areas declared 'disturbed' under the Armed Forces Special Power Act over the past 50 years vary significantly according to their conflict history, ethnic constituency, and levels of militancy. However, all these areas share a common experience of widespread human rights abuses during the imposition of the AFSPA. Terrorism costs lives all over the world, almost everyday. Governments can and should lawfully protect their citizens against such threats of violence. But many governments use the threats of terrorism as an excuse to continue to violate human rights, or create a climate of fear in which they can repress legitimate dissent and opposition. The AFSPA has also had the opposite effect to that intended by the Indian Government: in each State where the AFSPA has been implemented and soldiers have been deployed; the armed forces have become a symbol of oppression and an object of hate.

The sweeping monopoly over violence given to the armed forces under the Armed Forces Special Power Act is indeed made legitimate by the constitutional law, and in fact, several challenges in the court of law have been struck down, yet in the eyes of the conscientious citizenry not just in Manipur, but also in the rest of the country and indeed the world, the AFSPA is a gross transgression of the universal sense of moral legitimacy. This is, we would say, an aberration, but apart from such overkills, the notion of legitimate violence and the need for the State to exercise monopoly over it cannot be any better highlighted than in the situation of Manipur where unspeakable and murderous violence have become a part of everyday life. Practically, everybody with gun and commands violence is now justifying their brand of violence as legitimate skewing up the very idea of legitimacy. By contrast, the State which is supposed to exercise this monopoly, is neither able to meet the challenges from non-state power centres or keep within what the law prescribes as its limits of the exercise of legitimate violence. The rising cases of custodial deaths of prisoners are just the most recent and prominent examples.

The recent developments in Manipur in this regard have been nothing, but depressing. The masses have withdrawn into their shells, hounded into submission and cowardice by decades of atrocities and intimidation against the exercise of their free will and moral judgement on issues of gravity of the State, by the State and increasingly now, the non-State challengers to the State power. This is unfortunate for it can spell the ultimate doom of the quality of the character of the people here, who once prided themselves for their uncompromising independence and courage in chalking out the blueprints of their individual and collective futures.

The State actors are so powerful on the bases of the instructions of the Government with different Acts and Laws. At the same time, the non-state actors are also so powerful with their guerilla war tactics. No civilian has the power to raise any question against the activities of the non-state actors. Only women and women groups raise their heads in certain cases with their motherly feelings/spirit. An academic study on women is quite comprehensive. Mainly in the study of behavioural sciences, to come to the generalization is a very difficult job. Again, the interpretation of the problems and issues that are happening in almost all the societies are also quite different. But one similarity we find so far is women who constitute nearly half of the total population have been subjugated by men ever since the beginning of her creation. Despite of all the material progress of the modern era, the status of women has changed very little. Though there are a lot of talks about women empowerment, yet the true empowerment is still far from reality, as is evident from increasing rape cases and brutality shown against them every now and then. Only at late, after the brutal rape case of 16th December (Nirbhaya), we have been shaken out of slumber and our Government hastily enacted a law, in the form of an ordinance based on Justice J.S. Verma Committee recommendations, thus, doing a marathon job spurt by the urgency of circumstances. But, as a matter of fact, Nirbhaya rape case was not the single brutal action of violence against women; there are a number of cases which are not noticed/hardly noticed to the public. The case of

Nirbhaya was exposed just within one year (nine months only), but the case of the custodial rape and killing of Ms. Thangjam Manorama Devi of Imphal East District of Manipur (July 14, 2004) has been sleeping more than 10 years. Her parents are waiting for the judgement. There are number of cases which are not taking the shelter of the law of the country or not known to the public due to fear psyche or stigma concerns too. Such cases of serial sexual offences happen not only in our country, but also have been reported from different parts of the world. A slow and tedious legal process in our country further increases the problem.

Modern society seems to be seen as womenliness subjected to processes of hegemonization and homogenization as the national culture seek to stake its identity. The mass media, whether controlled by the State or subjected to the demands of the market mechanism, have been the active instruments of this transformation. In a sense, the commoditization of women through advertisement is implicit in the function of display, but it is made explicit by the consociation of images of women with a range of material products, rather after the manner of commercial advertizing. Commercial advertising uses essentially the same language and also exploits images of women and displays of women's bodies, whether or not the product concerned is gender-typed. The consociation of women with material products has two distinct, but related functions. On the one hand it reinforced cultural stereotypes of women's roles with particular stress on the domestic roles. The constant reiteration of certain associations has the ideological function of making gender roles constructed culturally appear as natural and consumer products concerned naturally and self-evidently feminized. The housewife is surrounded by a set of modern kitchen appliances, or is seen busily at work on her sewing machine etc.

Post-modernism made a drastic shift in the concept of power and the shift was from sovereignty to Governmental rationality—from supra-legal sovereignty to the multiplicity of agents governing the society. Post-modernism is characterized—juridical—discussion conception of power and shifts the focus of the State from being a disciplinary power towards being a bio-power. There has been a shift in the search from the state based power structure to the wider society based power structure. This shift has been visible in recent times particularly with the emergence of civil society institutions which seek to relocate power in the milieu of the society where the role of social agencies, civil society organizations, especially women organizations, and community organizations are considered more significant then that of the State in redefining and relocating power relations. Micro-social movements emerged in different regions and states of the whole Indian subcontinent took various forms, including civil society movements, ethnic movements, women movements and so on. These movements trivialized the empowerment and emancipator consciousness of all sections of people and assumed strong depoliticized features.

The democratic model did not develop theoretically in most of the Third World countries till only after gaining Independence from colonial powers. The structure of political life for the ordinary women has largely remained hidden in the private sphere. Many feminists feel that democracy has failed to recognize women as political citizens in its theory and practice, and it has been more rewarding towards men than women. Third World women's liberation movements often have their origins in the national liberation movements. When the women entered into the socio-political process of the country, they started to take over the right, justice, equality etc. They set down some basic norms like, equal rights and obligation for all Indian citizens without sex bar; no disability to any citizen because of religion, caste, creed, or sex in regard to public appointment to an office of power, adult suffrage, women to contest an equal terms with men in mixed general election etc. In a modern Parliamentary democratic form of Government, the study of electoral politics is the backbone of the social science studies. The common factors which support the exclusion of women in the electoral politics are—socio-cultural factors including the ideological factors and lack of social capital; political factors including political structure, institution and functional constraints and lack of political capacity; and economic factors. The extension of her activities and specially her involvement in politics creates within the Gandhian ideology an irresolvable tension. For politics, one cannot be restricted necessarily to the home. Gandhiji builds a new model of Indian women dedicated to the service of the nation. However, she can perform this role only if she turns her back on sex, reproductive and social aspects of relationship between male and female which defines their separate spheres in modern Indian life and yet creates a space for a women involved in public life after rejecting the Gandhian notions of feminity and womenhood. On the one hand is the construction of a morally superior women, a loving wife and a dedicated mother, involved actively in the making-the-nation, spinning *khadi*, sharing equal task in the house with the male, and on the other a reconstruction of a de-sexed women, who has sacrificed her reproductive aspects, her family life and has dedicated herself to the service of the nation. So, in a Parliamentary democratic system, political participation of women got a number of questions like what, when, how etc., but they are so advance in participatory democracy in Gandhian model. When a political struggle in the land assumed popular character, it was inevitable that Manipuri women should ferment the dough with the yeast of their militancy. Yet, the civil society protest movements organized by the women from time-to-time against unjust Government decisions have impacted on the State policy in respect of human liberty. This may be reckoned as a significant feature of women power in Manipur. And the women of Manipur should actively deliberate on how they may be able to assert their rights in the political decision-making system.

Under liberal constitutionalism the aspirational politics in different parts of the country delved into the concept of ethnic States (state reorganization) as a countervailing institution to the hegemonic and powerful nation-state. The movements for the same were expressed in multiple ways ranging from secession, political bargaining and compromise—in all which women took part without considering their status, power, privilege and consequences—although the polarization between the State hegemony and the ethnic questions could hardly be happily reconciled. Things became more confounded with the multiple events taking place in different States of India under the liberal constitutionalism. Regulatory democratic legislation, introduction of Autonomous District Councils in the Tribal Areas, Politics of Accord etc. mentioned nothing about women (which women can come out from the traditional power structure of the Chieftainship organizations).

We can find women in different forms—from rulers and warriors to sportswomen and innovators, and from writers and artists to heroines and revolutionaries, these are moving accounts of struggle, tragedy, dedication and triumphs, more dramatic than any fiction. Progressing through history each of these exceptional women's role/stories is told against the backdrop of their time. For each, we learn of their achievements, backgrounds, characters, and little known details that make them ever more remarkable. Perhaps, in the land of Chitrangada and Rani Gaidinliu, a woman militant; Saroj Nalini Parrat, a woman educationist; Sharmila, a human rights activist; and Mary Kom, a pugilist—is nobody in particular. It is true that traditionally the Meitei women's political status as such and the scope for their formally taking part in the decision-making process and in the affairs of the government as well as their rights in sharing the inheriting property did not commensurate with the vital role played by them in economic and cultural sphere. They are playing a vital role in the economic and cultural sphere of Manipur, but that situation has not resulted in the women acquiring absolute equality with men which they more than deserve. Manipur remains as much a man's world as it ever was.

Development cannot take place unless the people at the grassroots level are not involved in the developmental programme. According to the modern point of view the objectives of business is to discharge its moral responsibility towards all the parties concerned and also earn profits simultaneously. But, while we examine into depth, conditions are quite challenging in case of north-eastern region of India. This is mainly due to the fact that, the Government of India is busier looking at the region through the lens of strategic importance and law and order issues and has ignored the combination of factors such as unchecked illegal migration, encroachment of land by immigrants and flaws of centrally administered policies that stripped the tribal village units of their sovereignty.

The main features of Indian Civilization focused the non-coercive nature, political hegemony, mendicantism, national political control, tributary mode of governance within the federal structure and predominance/disguise of customary laws. The liberal democratic Constitution of India opened up the floodgate and the women were empowered to take in the socio-economic and political processes. They could to some extent position themselves in the political spheres at different levels, though this could not substantially reverse the existing status of the women in this country. While it is very important to involve them in the process of development, provision of liberty, equality with equity, and justice, and to understand the interrelations between development and power relationship of all sections of people. In this globalized world, the magnitude of cross border activities in finance and industry has become so great that States' regulatory leverages have virtually disappeared. In this situation, the boundaries between countries remained clear on a political map, but those boundaries have disappeared on the economy and financial relations. Through competition, imitation, and diffusion of best practices, trade, and capital mobility, globalization is said to produce convergence across nations both in the structures of production and in the relations among economy, society, and the State. Trade liberalization opening up markets to the free flow of goods and services was supposed to lead to growth. The evidence is not clear. It is a mixed one. In some part international trade is not successful in promoting growth in poor countries as they are often unbalanced. The advanced industrial countries were allowed to levy tariffs on goods produced by developing countries that were, on average, four times higher than those on goods produced by other advanced industrial countries. It is quite failed to the poor marginalized section of people. This can easily be exhibited with the women of north-east India. Open competition to all is the most fundamental behaviour in the global economy. New markets, new alliance and new customers are emerging daily in different parts of the globe. So, our business needs to define for itself a global vision and development strategies in coherence with this vision. Meanwhile, women are far shy for competition in this new changing scenario, far legging behind the global players in terms of technology application, skill and experience in various allied fields such as management, production and marketing. They are still tradition and culture bound.

The problems and issues of the society started right from the family level and involved the whole human environment and again affected the entire civil society in which women are not excluded. Because of gender sensitization, women got themselves involved in different kinds and types of movements, either to express their views and opinions or free themselves from the numerous shackles of life as well as to protect and safeguard their dignity as women. On the bases of these issues and other facts of life, today women are no longer remained within the confines of tradition, custom and culture inherited by generation after generations. They moved out or are forced to do so to find ways and means to improve their status by deciding for themselves and do not wait any longer for others to decide their future; and not only for themselves they could not remain as a mere spectator in this decaying social scenario. Their areas of activities and actions spread far and wide, and because of this, the civil society can no longer remain as an onlooker to the women's issues and problems; it has to address and listen to their opinions and expressions. Sometimes, the issues of women and their movements are politicized by political and social elites according to their needs. Marginalization of women and feminization of poverty are now at the centre stage on women issues. This arises from the increasing proportion of women among the poor due to several factors. These factors are insecure land tenure, poor access of basic social needs like leisure, health, sanitation, and education and effects of various forms of discrimination against women.

Education is not simply about jobs. Education is also about access to new knowledge, information and ideas as well as the capacity to use these effectively. These are enhancements of the capabilities that individuals bring to their goals in many areas of life, aside from the labour market. They explain some aspects of the correlation between women's education and various human development outcomes. There are lessons to be learnt from studies which demonstrate that access to particular resources have helped women to empower themselves. At the same time, there are also lessons to learn from studies that suggest the reverse. Unpacking these different outcomes to look at underlying causes draws attention to the social relationships through which they were brought about.

Women experienced gender subordination/discrimination in a complex manner in any society even though the degree may be different. Women may not necessarily be aware of, or desire to realize, their 'strategic' gender interests. This may arise out of women's socialization into patriarchy, thus creating in them a 'false consciousness'. Or, it may be that the restriction on their mobility and experience prevent them from knowing other ways of being. Or, they may be aware of the circumscribed nature of their lives without knowing what to do about it. The democratic government has been trying to create favourable changes in the socio-economic and political atmosphere and making them capable citizens of the State to discharge their duties in a positive and rightful manner. Women who were subjected to various kinds of subordination and inferiority position due to traditional social norms, beliefs and practices, handed down from generation to generation depicting gender roles are called for to empower themselves from within and from the laws, enactments, policies framed by the government. Democracy promised them the enjoyment of equal political rights with men as candidates as well as voters in the electoral process and equal participation in the decision-making process of the State. But in all democratic countries of the world, women participating in the decision-making process are found to be less than men. The question is how this happens after so many Acts, laws, regulations, covenants, conventions etc. which are trying to make women equal with men in their respective constitutions. There still exists a big gap between what is written in the Constitution and various laws passed by the Governments and what is prevailing in practice.

In the spheres of social and household relations the important task is to raise the social awareness by continuous exhortation. Every person in the society and in the family has to be aware of the rights, needs, well and woes, pleasure and pain as well as honour and dignity of the women. When women became the decision-makers or at the managerial position, they would be able to break the glass ceiling around them and to create women friendly environment. Women in such position would also help to bring about change in attitude, beliefs and thoughts and in enhancing motivation and self-confidence among them. As the wearer knows where the shoe pinches clearly, women acknowledged their problems very clearly. So, women have to organize themselves to assert their rights and extract their rights. Decentralized democratic administration is the most useful mechanism to empower women. In the social life the bias against women and girl child in spite of the efforts made by the Government and Non-governmental organizations has to be fought by social movements and by ensuring freedom to women from the oppressive social codes. Both men and women will have to work together in this direction so that human resources are not wasted or exploited by the brutal forces.

Bibliography

Books

Agarwal, R.C., 1987, *Indian Government and Politics*, S. Chand & Company Pvt. Ltd., New Delhi.

A.H. Doctor, 1985, *Issues of Political Theory*, Sterling Publication, New Delhi.

Anjali Gandhi (ed.), 2006, *Women's Work, Health and Empowerment*, Aakar Books, Delhi.

Andal, N., *Women and Indian Society-option and Constraints*, Rawat Publication, Jaipur.

Basu, Durga Das, *Shorter Constitution of India*, Prentice Hall of India Pvt. Ltd., New Delhi.

B. Pakem, 1997, *Insurgency in North-East India*, Omson Publication, New Delhi.

B.K. Ahluwalia, Shashi Ahluwalia, 1984, *Social Change in Manipur*, Cultural Publishing House, Delhi.

Bose, Anima, 1991, *Peace and Conflict Resolution in the World Community*, Vikas Publishing House Pvt. Ltd., New Delhi.

C. Joshwa Thomas, R. Gopalkrishna and R.K. Ranjan Singh (eds.), *Constraints in Development in Manipur*, Regency Publication, New Delhi.

Constantile, R., *Manipur Maid of the Mountains*, Lancers Publisher.

Chanda, Anuradha; Sarkar Mahua, Chattopadhyay, 2003, *Women in History*, Progressive Publishers, Kolkata.

Chouhan, Laxmidhar, 2007, *Women and the Law*, Mittal Publication.

Chaube, S.K., 1985, *Electoral Politics in North-East India*, University Press, Madras.

Desai, A.R., 1986, *Social Background of Indian Nationalism*, Popular Prakashan, Bombay.

Dutta, P.S., 1986, *Electoral Politics in North-East India*, Omson Publication, New Delhi.

Fernandes, Walter; Bharali Gita; Kezo Vemedo, (eds.) 2007, *The UN Indegenous Decade in Northeast India*, North-Eastern Social Research Centre, Guwahati.

Fernandes, Walter (ed.), 2008, *Search for Peace with* Justice, *Issues Around Conflict in North-East India*, North-Eastern Social Research Centre, Guwahati.

Goswami, Roshni, Goswami Meghna and Sreekala, M.G., *Women in Armed Conflict Situation in North-East,* Network, N. Barooch Lane, Jorpukhuri, Guwahati, Assam.

Ghose, Chitra; Ray, Soma; Chande, Chandni (ed.) 2002, *Opening the Closed Windows,* Progressive Publishers, Kolkata.

Gassah, L.S. (ed.), 2008, *Women Empowerment Movement in North-East India,* Omson Publication, New Delhi.

G. Aloysius, 2004, *No Freedom with Caste, the Menace of Hindu Imperialism,* Media House, Delhi.

Horam, M., 2000, *The Rising Manipur, Including other North-Eastern States,* Manas Publication, New Delhi.

Hodson, T.C., 2007, *The Naga Tribes of Manipur,* Low Price Publication, New Delhi.

J.R. Kokandakar, 1994, *Prelude to the Search of Truth;* Bharatiya Vidya Bhavan, Bombay.

Karna, M.N., (Ed.), 1988, *Social Movements in North-East India,* Indus Publishing Company, New Delhi.

Krishna Mohan Mathur, *Crime, Human Rights and National Security;* Gyan Book Ltd., New Delhi.

Kalam, APJ Abdul, 2002, *Ignited Minds,* Penguin Books.

K.A. Kunjakan, 2002, *Feminism and Indian Realities,* Mittal Publication, New Delhi.

Karam, Manimohan Singh, 2006, *Nupilal* (Women's war of Manipur) K. Premlata Devi, Imphal.

Kapur, A.C., 1981, *Principles of Political Science,* S. Chand & Company Ltd., New Delhi.

Kshetri, Bimola, 2010, *Government and Politics in Manipur,* Ashangba Communications, Imphal.

Kaul, Vinita, *Women and the Wind of Change,* Gyan Books, New Delhi.

Moitra Shefali, *Women, Heritage and Violence,* Papyrus, Culcutta.

Madhushree Dutta, Elavia Agnes, Neera Adarkar (eds.), 1996, *The Nation, the State and Indian Identity,* Bhatkal Books International, Bombay.

Micheal, S. Kinnul, 2000, *The Gendered Society,* Oxford University Press, New York.

Neluka, Silva, 2004, *The Gendered Nation, Contemporary Writings from Asia;* Sage Publication, New Delhi.

Nuh, V.K., 2001, *Struggle for Identity in North-East India,* Spectrum Publication, Guwahati.

Panchani, Chandra Shekhar, *Manipur, Religion, Culture and Society,* Konark Publishers Pvt. Ltd.

Phanjoubam, Tarapot, *Bleeding Manipur,* Har Anand Publication Pvt. Ltd., New Delhi.

Roy, Ashini, 2003, *Violence Against Women,* Rajat Publication, New Delhi.

Ray, Asok Kumar and Chakraborty, Satyabrata, (eds.), 2008, *Society, Politics and Development in North-East India,* Concept Publishing Company Pvt. Ltd., New Delhi.

Ray, B. Dutta and Ray, Asok Kumar (eds.), 2008, *Women Emancipation, Focus on North-East India*, Om Publication, New Delhi.

Ray, B. Dutta and Ray, Asok Kumar (eds.), 2006, *Dynamics of Power Relations in Tribal Societies of North-East India*, Om Publication, New Delhi.

Ray, B. Dutta, Dev Bimal J. (eds.), 2008, *Globalization and North-East India*, Concept Publishing Company Pvt. Ltd., New Delhi.

Ray, B. Dutta, Sarma, Siddeshwar, Dev, Bimal J. (eds.), 2011, *Freedom Struggle in North-East India*, Omson Publications, New Delhi.

Ray, Vikas Narayan, (Ed.) *Larkiyon ka Inkilab Jindabad*, Sahitya Upakrama, Etihashbad Prakashan, Allahabad, 8th Edition, September 2009.

Ray, Asok Kumar and Dev, Bimal J. (eds.), 2007, *Terrorism and Human Rights in North-East India*, Om Publication, New Delhi.

Sarkar, Aanchal, 2006, *Gender and Development*, Pragun Publication, New Delhi.

Satish Chandra, *Civil and Political Rights of the Aliens—A study in National and International Laws*, Deep and Deep Publication, New Delhi.

Siddiqi, Fatima Ehtasham and Ranganathan, Sarala, 2001, *A Guide for Social Activists*—Part I and Part II, Kanishka Publishers and Distributors, New Delhi.

Singh, L. Ibungohal, 1960, *An Introduction To Manipur*, Imphal.

Singh, N. Ibobi, 1976, *Manipur Administration*, 1707-1907, Imphal.

Singh, P. Bharat, 1997, *Elections in Manipur*, P. Mirabai Devi, Imphal.

Singh, R.P., 1981, *Electoral Politics in Manipur*, Concept Publishing Company Pvt. Ltd., New Delhi.

Tandon, R.K., 1996, *Women-Nature, Education, Teaching and Rights*, Commonwealth Publishers, New Delhi.

Th. Binarani Devi, 2011, *Women's Movement in Manipur*, Concept Publishing Company Pvt. Ltd., New Delhi.

Th. Binarani Devi and K. Kunjani Devi (eds.), *Society and Politics in Manipur*, Birkunsam, Imphal.

Thorner, Alice and Maithrayi Krishnaraj, (eds.) 2000, *Ideas, Images and Real Lives*: Orient Longman Ltd., Bombay.

Tyagi, Suresh Kumar, 2012, *Human Rights and Democratization*, Swastic Publications, Delhi.

Journals

Economic and Political Weekly, Bombay.

Himalayan Journal of Contemporary Research, Shimla, Himachal Pradesh.

India Journal of Development Research, Institute of Development Studies, Varanasi.

Indian Journal of Social Science and Sciences, Sivasagar, Assam.

International Journal of English Language, Literature and Humanities (IJELLH), Bhopal, Madhya Pradesh.

International Journal of Interdisciplinary and Multidisciplinary (IJIMS) Vol. 1, No. 4.

Journal of International Academic Research for Multidisciplinary (JAIRM), Vol. 2, Issue 1.
Journal of North-East India Council for Social Science Research, Shillong, Meghalaya.
SKWC Journal of Social Sciences, S. Kula Women's College, Nambol, Manipur.
The Indian Journal of Political Science, Volume LXX, No. 1.

Newspapers

(a) National

Amrita Bazar Patrika, Kolkata.
Hindustan Times, New Delhi.
The Hindu.
The Statesmen, Kolkata.
The Times of India, Guwahati, Assam.

(b) Local

Huiyen Lanpao, (Manipuri), Imphal.
Mannaba (Manipuri), Imphal.
Naharolgi Thoudang (Manipuri), Imphal.
Poknapham, (Manipuri), Imphal.
Prajatantra, (Manipuri), Imphal.
The Imphal Free Press (Manipuri), Imphal.
The Sangai Express, (Manipuri), Imphal.
Yakairol, (Manipuri), Imphal.

Reports

Amnesty International India, 2004.
Amnesty International Report 2007.
Human Development Report 2005.

Documents

Domestic Violence Act, 2005.
Human Rights Watch, August 2008.
Manipur Constitution Act, 1948.
Office Record of the Manipur State Human Rights Commission.
Record of the Manipur State Commission for Women.

Index